QUICK AFTER-WORK
ENTERTAINING

Quick After-Work
ENTERTAINING

Hilaire Walden

PIATKUS

First published in 1996 by
Judy Piatkus (Publishers) Ltd
5 Windmill Street, London W1P 1HF

The moral right of the author has been asserted
*A catalogue record for this book is available from
the British Library*

ISBN 0-7499-1663-X

Designed by Paul Saunders
Illustrations by Madeleine David
Photographs by Steve Baxter
Home economy by Meg Jansz
Styling by Marian Price

Data capture by Selwood Systems, Midsomer Norton
Printed and bound in Great Britain by
Butler & Tanner Ltd, Frome and London

Contents

Introduction

As NICE as it may be to have plenty of time to spend cooking really special dishes for dinner parties, the reality is that, all too often, dinner parties are arranged for a weekday, when everything has to be done quickly after work. Through experience, I have found that if the evening and food are to be a success and I am not to be exhausted and flustered, I have to spend a little time thinking about and planning the menu and meal in advance. Of course, if the occasion is a last-minute, spontaneous one, this cannot be done, but if you are used to doing it, organising and cooking a dinner with relative ease will become more automatic.

Planning the Menu

Unless you are a very experienced cook and give dinner parties frequently or have an instinct for such things, when you are giving a dinner party spend a few minutes, quiet ones if possible, thinking about what you are going to serve, and planning the shopping and cooking. This way you are more likely to serve a balanced meal that you have cooked easily, and so will feel relaxed and able to enjoy the party.

The following points are not in order of importance and, although the list might look dauntingly long, it covers things which are fairly obvious as well as those that are less obvious.

1. As time is short, keep the meal simple. This doesn't mean that you have to serve very expensive luxuries like caviare, but you do need to choose ingredients wisely, going for quality and freshness.

2. Avoid serving more than one very rich or creamy dish in a meal.

3. Select dishes that provide some colour contrast. Vichyssoise, a creamy

chicken dish accompanied by cauliflower and rice, followed by meringues and cream is a classic example of what to avoid.

4. Think about the textures of the foods so the meal provides some things that are crisp, some crunchy ones, some that are soft and smooth and some that have 'bite'.

5. Balance the flavours and try not to have dishes that provide too many conflicting flavours, or that are too highly seasoned.

6. Look for any similarity of ingredients, such as fruit in succeeding courses, and change one of the dishes.

7. Choose fruit, vegetables and some fish when they are in season because that is when they are at their best.

8. Choose dishes that are appropriate to the season. Lighter dishes are usually preferred to heavy or rich ones in the summer.

9. Make sure all the dishes can practically be cooked for the same meal. Avoid too many dishes that require last-minute attention, especially for the main course and its accompaniments. It is a wise idea to choose at least one course that can be prepared easily, then left while you get on with the rest of the meal. Sometimes parts of recipes can be prepared in advance.

10. Dishes that are cooked in the oven usually require less attention than those that are grilled or fried. If you are using the oven for one dish, try to choose one or two others, perhaps an accompaniment, that also require the oven.

11. When I am cooking a meal for someone, I want to give them something they will enjoy and do not want to cause them any embarrassment, so I always ask guests if there are any foods they prefer not to eat. This saves any awkwardness, and perhaps having frantically to rustle up something different. However, if there is one vegetarian in a party of six, I do not make the other five eat a vegetarian meal. I select a first course that is acceptable to everyone and prepare in advance a non-meat alternative main course and put it on the table as inconspicuously as possible. Some people say they are vegetarian when in fact they eat fish and chicken, so it's worth making clear what someone means.

Planning, Cooking and Serving the Meal

The following is a list of general points to help you get organised, and to keep calm. More specific advice is given in the recipe and chapter introductions throughout this book.

1. Make lists of what you have to buy, and when.

2. Work out a plan of action on as large a piece of paper as possible, keeping the points brief and highlighting the most vital parts.

3. When working out the times when you need to start cooking items, don't forget that water will take longer to come to the boil in winter, and that it takes a surprisingly long time for a saucepan to return to the boil after vegetables for six people have been added. To cut this time down as much as possible, have as much water in the pan as you can, without it spilling.

4. Do as much shopping as possible in advance, but not at the expense of losing quality in perishable items such as fish and leafy vegetables. Meat can be bought a day or two in advance. Large pieces keep better for longer than individual cuts. Unwrap the meat, put it on a plate, cover it with clingfilm and store it in the coldest part of the refrigerator.

5. Prepare ahead as much as you can.

6. Lay the table the night or morning before.

7. Get out as many of the ingredients and equipment as is sensible, and keep them in the appropriate groups.

8. Don't forget to turn the oven on in advance.

9. Remember to warm the plates and appropriate serving dishes for all courses that are to be served hot. If there isn't room in the oven or under the grill, put them over a saucepan of boiling water.

10. To save clutter and a sink piled high with dirty dishes, and nowhere left to put the next batch as they come from the dining-room, I put ready a large bucket of hot soapy water.

Quick Cooking Tips

I have given hints and tips for cooking quickly in my other Quick-After Work cookbooks, and I apologise to readers who have those books, but I am going over those points again because I hope they will help those readers who do not have the other books (there are probably more of them than those who do, and I trust the latter group will be sufficiently happy with the new recipes not to mind).

- Read through your chosen recipes carefully to make sure you have all the ingredients and equipment required, and to check that it is physically possible to cook and serve the recipes together to make a meal that can be cooked easily. Also, having a reasonably good idea of what needs to be done when cooking a dish will save you having to refer to the recipe repeatedly, so saving time.

- Put any dishes or ingredients that need to be chilled into the refrigerator. (If you forget to do this, you can always pop them into the freezer for a short while, but don't forget they are there.)

- Take out any ingredients that are in the fridge at least 30 minutes before using them. Cold ingredients take longer to cook than those at room temperature. The temperature of equipment will also affect how long food takes to cook. For example, if you bake Cheese Puffs (see page 13) in soufflé dishes that have been kept in a cold cupboard rather than one at normal, or perhaps slightly warm, room temperature, the Puffs will need a longer cooking time because not only will the dishes take longer to heat through, but they will cool down the Puff mixture and lower the oven temperature more when they are put in.

- Remember that small pieces cook more quickly than large ones.

- Dice butter before melting it so that it melts more quickly.

- Young vegetables cook more quickly than older ones, not only because they are smaller but because they are more tender.

- At least one good quality sharp knife will save time and can improve the appearance of cut foods.

- Although ovens have thermostats, they are notoriously inaccurate. I therefore have an oven thermometer almost permanently in my oven so I know that all the oven temperatures I give in my recipes are correct. I suggest that you get an oven thermometer; they don't cost much and if you are bothering to cook a meal for a special occasion or for some other reason, when you particularly want it to turn out well, the outlay is well worth it.

- Ovens take different times to preheat. Mine, an ordinary gas cooker converted to LPG (liquid petroleum gas such as Calor gas) takes only 5 minutes to reach 180°C/350°F/gas 4 and 7–8 minutes to get to 200°C/400°F/gas 6. Check how long it takes your oven to heat up. As opening the door and putting in cold dishes lowers the temperature in the oven, if there is time it can be worth preheating the oven to a slightly higher temperature than is required for cooking.

Ingredients

Although the recipes cover a wide range of different styles of cooking and use ingredients from many different countries, none of them are difficult to find and should be obtainable in good supermarkets. When entertaining, use the best quality of all the ingredients that you can afford; even one poor-quality ingredient can spoil a dish and override the fact that you have spent more money on the other ingredients. For example, a harsh, cheap vinegar in a salad dressing can detract from an expensive, good quality olive oil.

A reasonably well stocked store-cupboard and fridge will save you shopping time on the occasions when you have a lot of things to buy. Take time when you are not cooking for a special occasion to find good-quality branded products; quality is not always related to price.

BUTTER

I always use unsalted butter because it may well be fresher than salted butter and so tastes better.

OILS

I use a mild olive oil for general cooking and recipes where I do not particularly want to taste the oil. For salad dressings and recipes where the flavour of the oil is part of the overall blend of flavours, I use virgin or extra-virgin olive oil. Exceptions are Far Eastern dishes; for these, ground-nut (peanut) oil may be more appropriate for frying, with sesame oil for a distinctive flavour. There are two types of sesame oil – light and dark. The light has less flavour and can be used for frying. Dark sesame oil is made from roasted sesame seeds and so has a rich flavour. It is used with discretion like a seasoning.

FLAVOURED OILS

It is easy to make your own flavoured oils for adding to cooking and dressings. Simply half fill a bottle or jar with fresh herbs, or add a chosen spice such as a few chillies, and fill the bottle or jar completely with mild olive oil. Put on the lid and leave for 2–4 weeks, shaking occasionally.

PASTRY

Puff and, especially, filo pastries are difficult to make so commercial packs of ready-made fresh or frozen pastry are a godsend. (It's even possible to buy ready-rolled sheets of puff pastry.) I always keep a pack of both types in the freezer.

SOY SAUCE

There are two types of soy sauce. Light soy sauce, which is the one most often used, especially with light meats, is less salty than the dark variety. This is also sweeter and thicker, and is used for dipping sauces.

VEGETABLES

Self-service selection has meant that you can be as fussy as you like over the vegetables you choose without being made to feel you are being a nuisance. Vegetables in their correct season will have more flavour and may keep better. All vegetables should be bright and free of bruises, cuts, mould or diseased patches. Leafy vegetables and salads, fennel, asparagus and root vegetables should be crisp, not limp. The top and underside of mushrooms should be dry. Root vegetables can be bought a day or two in advance and kept in a cool place. If they are packed in a plastic bag make sure there are holes in it, or untie the top. Remove mushrooms from plastic bags or remove the cling film covering of plastic trays. Wrap or cover the mushrooms with paper and keep in the refrigerator.

VINEGARS

Vinegars vary in quality and therefore harshness. Good wine vinegars, both red and white, are as essential as a good olive oil. On the whole, French wine vinegars are better than their English equivalents; the best come from Martin Pouret because it is the only company still making vinegar in the traditional way, i.e. ageing it in oak barrels. They are available from good supermarkets and delicatessens, and Crabtree & Evelyn.

Balsamic vinegar has recently sprung to popularity. Very old balsamic vinegars have such an intense, sweet flavour that they are used very sparingly, more like a seasoning than a vinegar. They are also very expensive. Younger, more commercial vinegars lack the character of the older types, but they still have a distinctive, sweet taste. They can be used more lavishly.

Sherry vinegar also has a rich flavour, but not the sweetness of balsamic. It has a sherry-like flavour, which is not surprising as it is aged in a succession of barrels in the same way as sherry.

As with oils, it is very easy and inexpensive to make your own flavoured vinegars for instantly adding variety and interest to dressings.

WINE

It is a false economy to think you can get away with using a cheap, inferior wine or the accumulated dregs of bottles for cooking. Whatever a wine tastes like before cooking, it will taste just as bad, or even worse, after cooking, so instead of adding quality to a dish, it will spoil it. The usual recommendation is to use the same wine as you will be drinking with a dish. If the table wine is quite expensive and you would prefer to use something cheaper, use one with the same basic style – a not-too-full-flavoured cabernet sauvignon, for example, rather than an expensive claret.

The body of a wine influences the effect it has on a dish so I generally use medium-bodied (by which I do not mean medium-sweet or medium-dry) wines. A thin muscadet will not produce such a tasty sauce as a chardonnay.

Menus

Pumpkin and Ginger Soup
Cornmeal Muffins

*

Pork Collops with Artichokes and Mushrooms

*

Coconut Custards

Light Crab Salad

*

Baked Duck Breasts with Tropical Salsa

*

Ginger Pots

Spinach, Pecorino Cheese and Almond Salad

*

Italian Roast Chicken and Vegetables
Broccoli with Olive Oil Hollandaise Sauce

*

Plum Tart

Baby Brioches with Prawns

*

Partridge with Mushrooms

*

Mango and Banana Fool

Mango Vinaigrette

*

Baby Salmon with Fennel Mayonnaise
Golden Potatoes

*

Soft Fruit Tart

Melon and Parma Ham Salad

*

*Sautéed Whole Fillet of Beef
with Chinese Marinade*

*

Chocolate Amaretto Castles

Cheese Puffs
or
Tomato and Thyme Tarts

*

Bass with Ginger Vinaigrette

*

Baked Buttery Spiced Bananas

Quick Crab Soufflés

*

Duck Breasts with Kumquats

*

Ginger Pots

Warm Prawn and Basil Salad

*

Pork Roulades with Feta and Herb Filling

*

Spiced and Buttered Plums

Proper Prawn Cocktail

*

Steaks with Béarnaise Sauce

*

Mango and Banana Fool

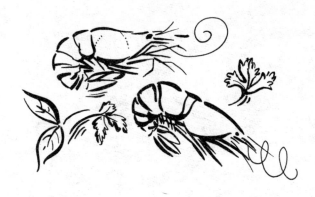

Light Crab Salad
or
Baby Brioches with Prawns

*

Poached Chicken Breasts with
Coriander and Ginger Mayonnaise

*

Plum Tart
or
Soft Fruit Tart

Crisp and Melting Tomato and Mozzarella Filo
Pastries

*

Spice-Encrusted Prawns

*

No-cook Dried Fruit Compote

First Courses

T HE FIRST course provides the welcome to the table and to the meal, and should stimulate the appetite. Appearance is particularly important, especially if the dish will be on the dining table when guests arrive at it. This doesn't mean you have to spend hours arranging and garnishing; even simple first courses such as Melon and Parma Ham Salad, can look inviting if they have been freshly prepared from fresh ingredients.

Soups are easy and useful because they can be left to cook and timing is not critical. Proper stock (not from a cube) is vital; if you don't make your own, which is by far the cheapest and does not require much skill or effort and can be kept in the freezer, fresh stocks are now available in the chiller cabinets of good supermarkets. Serving a bowl of hot home-made croûtons to sprinkle on the soup shows extra thought and trouble. When it is appropriate to the soup I toss the croûtons with finely grated cheese, sesame seeds or walnut, hazelnut or sesame oil. To eat with soup I either offer Cornmeal Muffins (see page 104) or bake some part-baked rolls; the smell of these is always appetising and fresh bread straight from the oven is always well received, even if the quality of this type of bread is not of the highest standard.

SPICED CARROT SOUP

·

—— SERVES 6 ——

IN WINTER, or on cool evenings in the spring and autumn, a creamy spiced (but not spicy) soup is most welcome. If you wanted to, you could prepare this soup up to the end of stage 3 in advance.

·

40g (1½oz) unsalted butter, diced
1kg (2lb) small carrots, sliced
1 garlic clove, crushed
1 bunch of spring onions, chopped
½ teaspoon ground ginger
½ teaspoon ground mace
½ teaspoon crushed coriander seeds

½ teaspoon ground coriander
1.4 litres (2½ pints) chicken or vegetable stock
150ml (5fl oz) crème fraîche or single cream
salt and freshly ground black pepper
coriander leaves for garnish

·

1. Heat the butter in a saucepan, add the carrots, garlic and spring onions, cover and cook gently for about 5 minutes.

2. Stir in the spices and cook for 1 minute. Add the stock and simmer, uncovered, for about 20 minutes or until the carrots are tender.

3. Allow to cool slightly, then purée in a blender.

4. Return the soup to the rinsed-out pan and reheat until almost boiling. Stir in the crème fraîche or single cream and seasoning. Serve garnished with coriander leaves.

PUMPKIN AND GINGER SOUP

·

—— SERVES 6 ——

IF YOU use a firm-fleshed pumpkin with a good flavour, such as butternut, rather than the traditional large British variety, the soup will have much more flavour. The amount of water that pumpkin produces is variable so it is not possible to specify how much stock will be needed. Be more generous with the butter if you would like a more buttery soup.

·

1 tablespoon olive oil
75g (3oz) unsalted butter
75g (3oz) piece of fresh root ginger, grated
900 g (2lb) firm pumpkin flesh, chopped

750ml–1.5 litres (1$\frac{1}{2}$–2$\frac{1}{2}$ pints) vegetable or
  chicken stock
salt and freshly ground black pepper

·

1. Heat the oil and half the butter in a saucepan, add the ginger and fry for 30 seconds. Stir in the pumpkin, cover tightly and cook over a low heat for 15 minutes.

2. Leave the pumpkin to cool slightly, then purée in a blender. Return to the pan and add enough stock to give the required consistency. Reheat and season to taste. Add the remaining butter just before serving.

THAI PRAWN AND MANGETOUT SOUP

•

— SERVES 4 —

THIS is one of the quickest and easiest soups to prepare, and makes an immediately interesting start to a meal.

1 tablespoon groundnut oil
2 × 7.5cm (3 inch) stalks of lemon grass, slit in half lengthways and thinly sliced
1 fresh red chilli, chopped
2 garlic cloves, crushed
5cm (2 inch) piece of fresh root ginger, thinly sliced
570ml (1 pint) coconut milk

300ml ($\frac{1}{2}$ pint) fish stock
1 tablespoon Thai fish sauce (nam pla)
1 teaspoon light soy sauce
225g (8oz) mangetout
350g (12oz) peeled cooked large prawns
2$\frac{1}{2}$ tablespoons coriander leaves
thinly sliced spring onions for garnish

1. Heat the oil in a saucepan, and stir in the lemon grass, chilli, garlic and ginger. Cook, stirring, for 1 minute, then add the coconut milk, stock, fish sauce and soy sauce. Simmer gently for 10 minutes.

2. While the soup is cooking, slice the mangetout. Add to the soup and simmer for 3 minutes.

3. Add the prawns, and heat through for about 2 minutes. Add the coriander leaves, and serve garnished with sliced spring onions.

ASPARAGUS SOUP

•

—— SERVES 6 ——

THIS soup makes a simple, elegant first course and, if made with fresh asparagus, a fairly extravagant one. However, asparagus trimmings or frozen asparagus can also be used. If using asparagus trimmings add them with the leeks and check the soup after puréeing it to see if it needs sieving (they may also need to be cooked for longer than 10 minutes at stage 3). For a change try using finely grated orange zest as a flavouring. Instead of, or as well as, garnishing the soup with asparagus tips you could use short, fine strips, or diced smoked salmon, cooked prawns or shrimps.

50g (2oz) unsalted butter
3 small leeks
2 smallish potatoes
1.4 litres (2½ pints) vegetable stock or
   water

675g (1½lb) asparagus
about 175ml (6fl oz) crème fraîche
salt and freshly ground white or black
   pepper

1. Melt the butter in a saucepan. Meanwhile, slice the leeks then add to the melted butter and cook until soft.

2. While the leeks are cooking, dice the potatoes.

3. Add the potato to the pan with the stock or water. Bring to the boil then cover and simmer for about 10 minutes until almost soft.

4. While the potato is cooking, chop the asparagus, reserving a few of the tips for garnishing if liked.

5. Add the asparagus to the pan and boil uncovered for about 5 minutes or until tender.

6. If garnishing the soup with reserved asparagus tips, cook them in boiling salted water for about 3 minutes until just tender. Drain well, return to the saucepan and put the lid on to keep warm.

7. Purée the soup in a blender. Return to the pan, add crème fraîche and seasoning to taste and heat through. Serve garnished with the asparagus tips, if liked.

SPINACH, PECORINO CHEESE AND ALMOND SALAD

·

—— SERVES 6 ——

PECORINO is a piquant sheeps' milk cheese produced in every region of southern Italy. The type most often seen in this country is Pecorino Romano; buy the best you can find. Be sure that the almonds are fresh and showing no signs of rancidity. This is an extremely quick salad to prepare, and the warm spiced nuts make it that little bit different.

225g (8oz) small fresh spinach leaves	pinch of chilli powder
75g (3oz) pecorino cheese	8 tablespoons olive oil
$1\frac{1}{4}$ teaspoons cumin seeds	150g (5oz) blanched whole almonds
$\frac{3}{4}$ teaspoon ground turmeric	$1\frac{1}{2}$ tablespoons sherry vinegar
$1\frac{1}{4}$ teaspoons paprika pepper	salt and freshly ground black pepper

1. Divide the spinach leaves between four plates. Use a potato peeler to shave pecorino cheese over the spinach.

2. Heat a heavy-based frying pan, add the spices and heat until fragrant. Add 2 tablespoons of the oil and the almonds, and cook, stirring frequently, until the almonds are golden. Remove from the heat.

3. Whisk the remaining oil with the vinegar and seasoning. Pour over the salads, then scatter the almonds on top and serve.

MELON AND PARMA HAM SALAD

•

— SERVES 6 —

I USE three different colours of melon in this salad. Not only does it make the dish look attractive, but it adds interest to the taste and texture.

½ honeydew melon
½ ripe Charentais melon
½ Ogen melon
2 bunches of watercress
6 thin slices of Parma ham

DRESSING
4 tablespoons lime juice

4 tablespoons mild olive oil, or
    safflower or sunflower oil
4 tablespoons walnut oil
1 teaspoon Dijon mustard
2 teaspoons clear honey
¼ teaspoon grated lime zest
salt and freshly ground black pepper

1. Whisk together the dressing ingredients.

2. Discard the seeds from the melons and slice the flesh. Using the point of a knife, cut off and discard the rind.

3. Discard the tough stalks from the watercress. Cut the ham into strips.

4. Put the watercress on a large plate, and spoon over some of the dressing. Arrange the melon and ham on top, and spoon over the remaining dressing.

MANGO VINAIGRETTE

•

—— SERVES 6 ——

THIS is a quick and easy dish to prepare and can be even better if prepared ahead of time so the flavours can develop (but they do not get hotter). Cover with cling film and keep in a cool place.

3 large ripe mangoes
4½ tablespoons good quality white wine
   vinegar
¾ teaspoon Dijon mustard

½ fresh red chilli, deseeded and finely
   chopped
125ml (4½fl oz) olive oil
salt and freshly ground black pepper

1. Peel the mangoes, slice the flesh off the stones, and divide between six plates.

2. Whisk the vinegar, mustard, chilli and salt together, then slowly pour in the oil, whisking all the time. Add black pepper to taste. Pour over the mangoes.

SMOKED CHICKEN AND MANGO SALAD

·

—— SERVES 4 ——

Fruits go well with smoked meats and I particularly like the combination of light smoked chicken and the rich fruitiness of mango. Watercress adds a good counterbalance of taste and texture.

·

2 ripe mangoes, peeled and sliced
1 small fresh red chilli, deseeded and
  chopped
2 tablespoons good quality white wine
  vinegar

50ml (2fl oz) olive oil
350g (12oz) smoked chicken breast
150g (5oz) watercress
salt and freshly ground black pepper

1. Put one of the mangoes, the chilli, vinegar, oil and seasoning into a blender and blend until smooth.

2. Thickly slice the chicken, then cut into pieces. Discard the tough stalks from the watercress.

3. Arrange the chicken, watercress and sliced mango on four plates and pour over the mango dressing.

SMOKED CHICKEN WITH FIGS

•

WHETHER you use green or black figs, they should be at their most succulent and flavourful in the late summer. Press them gently before buying them to check if they are ripe. If not, pass them by.

350g (12oz) smoked chicken breast	3 fresh ripe figs
3 tablespoons mild olive oil	salad leaves, such as corn salad, feuille de
3 tablespoons walnut oil	chêne and watercress
2 tablespoons white wine vinegar	salt and freshly ground black pepper
40g (1½oz) walnut pieces	

---

1. Thinly slice the chicken. Whisk together the oils, vinegar and seasoning. Coarsely chop the walnuts and mix into the dressing. Spoon half over the chicken and leave for 10 minutes.

2. Quarter the figs. Arrange a few salad leaves on each of six plates, and put the chicken on top. Add the fig quarters and spoon the remaining dressing over the chicken and figs.

SMOKED VENISON WITH CUMBERLAND SAUCE

·

—— SERVES 6 ——

HOMEMADE Cumberland sauce adds a touch of distinction to this very simple dish. The sauce needs to be made long enough in advance to give it time to cool. If there is any left, it will keep if you heat it until it melts, and then pour it into a small, clean jar and cover with a lid. You can vary the salad garnish by adding some blanched strips of red pepper for extra colour, or some peeled fresh walnuts in the autumn.

·

175g (6oz) sliced smoked venison
mixed salad leaves to serve

CUMBERLAND SAUCE
1½ large, juicy oranges
juice of 2 lemons

150ml (5fl oz) red port
225g (8oz) redcurrant jelly
½ teaspoon Dijon mustard
large pinch of grated fresh ginger
pinch of cayenne pepper
salt

·

1. To make the Cumberland sauce, pare the zest from the whole orange, taking care not to include any white pith. Cut into fine shreds. Squeeze all the orange juice.

2. Put all the sauce ingredients in a saucepan and heat gently, stirring, until the jelly has melted, then simmer for 10 minutes. Pour into a serving bowl and leave to cool.

3. Arrange the venison and salad leaves on six plates. Serve the Cumberland sauce separately.

WARM PRAWN AND BASIL SALAD

•

THIS recipe should take you less than 10 minutes from start to finish (but you could prepare the dressing in advance if liked). It should be served straight away.

•

mixed salad leaves, including rocket, corn
  salad, lollo rosso and frisée
3 tablespoons olive oil
600g (1¼lb) raw peeled king prawns

DRESSING
50g (2oz) sun-dried tomatoes in oil,
  drained

leaves from a small bunch of basil
2 tablespoons sherry vinegar
4 tablespoons walnut oil
salt and freshly ground black pepper

•

1. Put all the dressing ingredients in a blender and mix until combined.

2. Divide the salad leaves between six plates.

3. Heat the oil in a frying pan, add the prawns and stir-fry for 2 minutes. Remove the pan from the heat and stir in the dressing.

4. Spoon the prawns on to the plates, and pour the dressing over the prawns and leaves. Serve straight away.

CHEESE PUFFS

·

——— SERVES 4 ———

WONDERFUL appetising smells waft from the kitchen while these puffs are cooking. Like soufflés, the puffs will sink soon after they are removed from the oven so make sure your guests are seated by the end of the cooking time.

40g (1½oz) unsalted butter, diced
225ml (8fl oz) milk
100g (3½oz) Parmesan cheese, freshly grated
25g (1oz) plain flour
115g (4oz) Gorgonzola or Stilton cheese, crumbled or diced

3 eggs
good pinch of mustard powder or 2–3 teaspoons Dijon mustard
freshly ground black pepper

1. Preheat the oven to 190°C/375°F/gas 5. Generously butter four individual soufflé dishes and put on a baking sheet.

2. Gently heat the butter in the milk until the butter has melted.

3. Meanwhile, reserve about 1 tablespoon of the Parmesan cheese and mix the remainder with the flour. Remove the milk from the heat and immediately whisk in the cheese and flour mixture, whisking vigorously until the sauce has thickened and is smooth.

4. Return the pan to a low heat, add the Gorgonzola or Stilton cheese and whisk in until it has just melted. Remove the pan from the heat straight away and whisk in the eggs, one at a time. Season with mustard and black pepper.

5. Divide the mixture between the prepared dishes, sprinkle with the reserved Parmesan cheese and bake for 15–20 minutes or until well risen and golden but still slightly soft in the centre. Serve immediately.

CRISP AND MELTING TOMATO AND MOZZARELLA FILO PASTRIES

•

— SERVES 6 —

ONCE you get into the swing of preparing these pastries, they take only a few moments. The recipe actually makes 15 pastries so you will have three spares should they not all turn out as well as they should ... or for you to eat to boost your flagging energy while preparing dinner, or the next day!

250g (9oz) large, well-flavoured tomatoes
½ bunch of spring onions
2 tablespoons chopped basil
175g (6oz) mozzarella cheese
6 sheets of filo pastry, about 30 × 20cm
   (12 × 8 inches) each

50g (2oz) unsalted butter, melted
sesame seeds for sprinkling
salt and freshly ground black pepper

---

1. Preheat the oven to 180°C/350°F/gas 4. Chop the tomatoes, thinly slice the spring onions and mix together with the basil and seasoning. Drain and finely chop the mozzarella.

2. Stack two sheets of filo pastry together, brushing each with melted butter. Cut widthways into five strips. Put 1 tablespoon of the tomato mixture and 1 tablespoon of the cheese about 2.5cm (1 inch) from the narrow end of one strip. Fold the bottom left-hand corner over the filling to make a triangle, then fold the triangle over and over along the strip to make a neat package. Repeat with the remaining strips. Put on a baking sheet, brush with melted butter and sprinkle with sesame seeds. Repeat with the remaining sheets of filo pastry.

3. Bake the pastries for 10–15 minutes or until golden.

OPPOSITE: Salmon with Mint Vinaigrette (page 28)

TOMATO AND THYME TARTS

·

—— SERVES 4 ——

I USUALLY only make these tarts when there are four of us for dinner because that is all I can bake in one batch in my oven. I transfer the tarts that were on the bottom shelf to the top shelf to continue cooking while I am covering the other two tarts. I use fridge-cold butter and grate it on the coarse side of a grater.

·

2 sheets of ready-rolled puff pastry, each 20cm (8 inches) square
4 large, well-flavoured tomatoes
3 spring onions
Red Pepper Pesto (see page 99) or sun-dried tomato paste for spreading

about 25g (1oz) cold unsalted butter
about $\frac{1}{2}$ teaspoon chopped thyme
freshly ground black pepper
thinly shaved or coarsely grated pecorino or Parmesan cheese to serve

·

1. Preheat the oven to 230°C/450°F/gas 8. Cut two 10.5cm (4$\frac{1}{2}$ inch) circles from each pastry sheet and put on baking sheets. Prick the tops well with a fork and bake in the oven for about 8 minutes or until risen and golden.

2. Meanwhile, thinly slice the tomatoes and finely chop the spring onions.

3. Spread the pesto or sun-dried tomato paste thinly over each pastry circle, sprinkle over the spring onions and cover with overlapping tomato slices. Coarsely grate or finely flake the butter over the tomatoes. Sprinkle over the thyme and season with black pepper.

4. Return to the oven for 8–10 minutes or until the pastry edges are nicely browned. Sprinkle with the pecorino or Parmesan. If liked, return the tarts to the oven for a few minutes to melt the cheese completely.

OPPOSITE: Tomato and Thyme Tart (above)

ASIAN-INSPIRED PRAWN AND AVOCADO SALAD

•

— SERVES 4 —

THIS combination of prawns and avocado is quite unlike the clichéd prawn and avocado cocktail. Heating peppercorns and coriander seeds brings out their flavour; it only takes a few moments but if you feel really pressurised, crush them while still cold.

1½ teaspoons black peppercorns
1 tablespoon coriander seeds
1 fresh red chilli, deseeded and finely
  chopped
juice of 3 limes
350g (12oz) peeled cooked king prawns
1 bunch of spring onions

175g (6oz) cucumber
1 large avocado
salt
chopped coriander for garnish
warmed small naan breads to serve

---

1. Heat a dry, small, heavy-based frying pan, add the peppercorns and coriander seeds, and heat for about 30 seconds or until fragrant. Crush the peppercorns and seeds and put into a bowl with the chilli, lime juice, prawns and salt.

2. Thinly slice the spring onions and cucumber, and stir into the bowl.

3. Halve, stone, peel and chop the avocado and mix gently into the bowl. Cover and leave for 30 minutes, if possible.

4. Stir some chopped coriander into the salad just before serving with warmed naan bread.

PRAWN AND PAPAYA SALAD

·

—— SERVES 6 ——

THIS is a light and delicate first course that takes only a matter of moments to prepare.

350g (12oz) peeled cooked king prawns
2–3 ripe papayas (depending on size)
grated lime zest for garnish

DRESSING
1 large fresh red chilli

150ml (5fl oz) olive oil
2 tablespoons white wine vinegar
$1\frac{1}{2}$–2 tablespoons clear honey
4 tablespoons lime juice
salt

1. Chop the chilli, discarding the seeds. Put most of the chilli and the remaining dressing ingredients in a blender and mix until smooth. Finely chop the reserved chilli. Stir the prawns into the dressing.

2. Halve the papayas and peel them. Scoop out and discard the seeds. Thinly slice the flesh and arrange on six plates. Add the prawns and dressing. Sprinkle with the reserved chilli and grated lime zest.

LIGHT CRAB SALAD

•

—— SERVES 4 ——

A FRESH crab salad is always a treat but a traditional crab salad with mayonnaise, delicious as it is, can be a little heavy for a dinner party first course. So here is an equally delicious but much lighter salad. Fresh crab meat, rather than frozen, will make all the difference; I certainly wouldn't use canned crab meat for a dinner party.

450g (1lb) mixed fresh white and brown
  crab meat
2 tablespoons capers, chopped if large
8 French *cornichons* or 2 larger gherkins,
  finely chopped
1 large shallot, finely chopped
2 tablespoons finely chopped coriander
finely grated zest and juice of 2 limes

2 tablespoons mild olive oil
a few drops of Tabasco sauce
salt and freshly ground black pepper
lettuce and watercress leaves to serve
lime wedges and coriander sprigs for
  garnish

1. Stir all the ingredients, except the lettuce and watercress leaves, and the garnish, together with a fork until evenly combined.

2. Put some lettuce and watercress leaves on each of four plates. Spoon the crab mixture on to the plates and garnish with lime wedges and coriander sprigs.

PROPER PRAWN COCKTAIL

•

— SERVES 6 —

P RAWN cocktails came into fashion in the sixties, and since the seventies have been a cliché of steak house and similar establishment meals. But a prawn cocktail does not have to consist of watery frozen prawns coated in a thin sweet tomato dressing piled on to limp lettuce. It can be a real treat, like this recipe. Adjust the proportions of the dressing ingredients to suit your taste. If you would prefer to use peeled cooked prawns, buy 450g (1lb) large ones.

900g (2lb) king prawns in their shells
mixed salad leaves
lemon wedges to serve

DRESSING
225ml (8fl oz) mayonnaise

2–3 tablespoons sun-dried tomato paste
about 1 tablespoon lemon juice
4 tablespoons double cream, lightly
  whipped
a few drops of Tabasco sauce
salt and freshly ground black pepper

1. Dry-fry the prawns in a large frying pan until the shells turn pink. Reserve six, if liked, for garnish. When the remainder are cool enough to handle, peel them and, using the point of a sharp knife, slit along their backs and remove the dark thread.

2. To make the dressing, mix the mayonnaise, sun-dried tomato paste and lemon juice together, then lightly fold in the cream. Add Tabasco and seasoning to taste.

3. Divide the salad leaves between six plates. Add the prawns and spoon over the dressing. Garnish with the reserved prawns, if liked, and serve with lemon wedges.

QUICK CRAB SOUFFLÉS

•

—— SERVES 6 ——

For this recipe you need fresh crab meat that has been removed from the shell, but not 'dressed crab', which will have breadcrumbs and seasonings added. Brown meat is needed as well as white, both for flavour and to add moistness and to help hold the mixture together.

225g (8oz) mixed fresh white and brown crab meat

3 tablespoons crème fraîche

1½ tablespoons sun-dried tomato paste

2 tablespoons lemon juice

½ teaspoon grated lemon zest

3 large eggs, separated

100g (3½oz) fresh breadcrumbs from a tasty loaf, without crusts

a few drops of Tabasco sauce

2 tablespoons freshly grated Parmesan cheese

salt and freshly ground black pepper

---

1. Preheat the oven to 180°C/350°F/gas 4. Oil six 150ml (¼ pint) ramekin dishes and put on a baking sheet.

2. Mix together the crab, crème fraîche, sun-dried tomato paste, lemon juice and zest, and egg yolks.

3. Reserve about 3 tablespoons of the breadcrumbs and stir the remainder into the crab mixture. Add Tabasco sauce and seasoning to taste.

4. Whisk the egg whites until stiff, and fold into the mixture.

5. Divide the mixture between the ramekin dishes and sprinkle over the reserved breadcrumbs and the Parmesan. Bake for about 10 minutes or until well risen, golden and very lightly set in the centre. Serve immediately.

PRAWN PATTIES

•

COOKING the patties in the oven means they need less oil and are less demanding on your attention than if they were grilled or fried. They can be served with Red Pepper Pesto (see page 99), Red Pepper and Tomato Sauce (see page 96) or Spiced Avocado Sauce (see page 22).

2 tablespoons olive oil
1 large onion, finely chopped
1 garlic clove, finely crushed, optional
generous ½ teaspoon paprika pepper
450g (1lb) peeled cooked prawns

3 tablespoons chopped tarragon
1 large egg (size 1), beaten
7 tablespoons crème fraîche
75g (3oz) fresh white breadcrumbs
salt and cayenne pepper

1. Preheat the oven to 180°C/350°F/gas 4. Heat the oil in a frying pan, add the onion and garlic, if using, and fry until softened but not coloured. Stir in the paprika for 30 seconds.

2. Meanwhile, finely chop the prawns and mix with the remaining ingredients.

3. Stir the onion and garlic into the prawn mixture and form into 12 flat cakes about 2.5cm (1 inch) thick. Put on a lightly oiled baking sheet and bake for 10–15 minutes.

GRILLED PRAWNS WITH SPICED AVOCADO SAUCE

·

—— SERVES 6 ——

THE avocado sauce is made in the same way as mayonnaise, but it cannot be made in advance otherwise it will darken.

24–30 raw tiger prawns in their shells
3 garlic cloves, crushed
3 tablespoons extra-virgin olive oil
juice of 1 lemon
salt and freshly ground black pepper

SPICED AVOCADO SAUCE
1 large avocado
1 large (size 1) egg yolk
1¼ teaspoons Dijon mustard

1¼ teaspoons ground cumin
200ml (7fl oz) olive oil
125ml (4½fl oz) Greek yogurt
1 well-flavoured tomato, seeded and chopped
juice of 1 lime
a few drops of Tabasco sauce
salt and freshly ground black pepper
chopped coriander for garnish

1. With the point of a sharp knife, slit the prawns down their backs and remove the dark vein. Put them in a dish and add the garlic, oil, lemon juice and seasoning. Leave to marinate for 30 minutes, stirring occasionally.

2. To make the sauce, peel and stone the avocado, then purée the flesh in a blender with the egg yolk, mustard and cumin. With the motor running, slowly pour in the oil until the sauce is well emulsified. Pour into a bowl and stir in the yogurt until combined. Add the tomato and lime juice, and Tabasco sauce, salt and pepper to taste. Garnish with chopped coriander.

3. Preheat the grill. Remove the prawns from the marinade and grill until they turn bright pink. Serve with the sauce.

BABY BRIOCHES WITH PRAWNS

•

—— SERVES 6 ——

THERE are many uses for the brioche crumbs you will be left with after making this recipe – in desserts such as queen of puddings, as a coating for grilled or fried fish, fried with garlic, then mixed with chopped parsley and chilli and tossed with pasta, or in bread sauce.

•

6 small brioches
350g (12oz) peeled cooked prawns
4 tablespoons crème fraîche
1 tablespoon chopped basil

Sun-dried Tomato and Olive Butter (see page 34)
salt and freshly ground black pepper

•

1. Preheat the oven to 130°C/250°F/gas 1. Pull or cut the tops off the brioches and use a teaspoon to scoop out the centres of the brioches, taking care not to pierce the walls. Warm through in the oven.

2. Gently warm the prawns with the crème fraîche, basil and seasoning to taste; do not overheat.

3. Spread the butter generously inside the brioche shells and fill with the prawn mixture. Replace the tops and serve straight away.

PRAWN AND MONKFISH KEBABS WITH TOMATO AND AVOCADO SALSA

·

—— SERVES 6 ——

Don't be put off by the long list of ingredients needed for this recipe. The marinade is made from straightforward store-cupboard ingredients, and the salsa doesn't require anything unusual; both are quick and easy to assemble. Remove the fish skewers from the refrigerator as soon as you get home, turn them over in the marinade and leave at room temperature for up to 1 hour. If it will be longer than that before you cook them, return the skewers to the fridge until 1 hour before needed.

675g (1½lb) monkfish fillets, cut into 18 chunks
12 raw tiger prawns, peeled and deveined
salt and freshly ground black pepper
coriander sprigs for garnish

MARINADE
3 garlic cloves, crushed
1 teaspoon ground turmeric
1½ teaspoons ground coriander
¾ teaspoon ground cumin
¾ teaspoon chilli powder

1½ tablespoons sun-dried tomato paste
grated zest and juice of 1½ limes
115ml (4fl oz) olive oil

SALSA
1 ripe avocado
1 well-flavoured tomato, finely chopped
½ small red onion, finely chopped
grated zest of ½ lime
1½ tablespoons lime juice
3 tablespoons chopped coriander
salt and freshly ground black pepper

1. Thread the monkfish and prawns alternately on to six skewers.

2. Mix together all the marinade ingredients, pour over the fish and prawns, turn the skewers over, then cover and leave in the refrigerator during the day.

3. To make the salsa, stone, peel and finely chop the avocado, then mix with the remaining ingredients and seasoning.

4. Preheat the grill. Season the fish, then grill on an oiled grill pan for about 6 minutes, turning as necessary.

5. Serve the kebabs with some of the salsa placed beside each one. Garnish with coriander sprigs.

CARROT TIMBALES WITH QUICK GINGER HOLLANDAISE

•

—— SERVES 6 ——

To make this delightful first course look even more attractive, cook the carrot mixture in individual brioche moulds. Orange or lime juice can be substituted for the lemon juice, if liked.

675g (1½lb) young carrots, grated
1 leek or onion, sliced or chopped
40g (1½oz) unsalted butter
vegetable stock or water to cover
3 eggs
50ml (2fl oz) crème fraîche
squeeze of lemon juice
freshly chopped parsley
salt and freshly ground black pepper

QUICK GINGER HOLLANDAISE
   SAUCE
175g (6oz) unsalted butter
3 egg yolks
about 1½ tablespoons lemon juice
1½ tablespoons grated fresh ginger
salt and freshly ground black pepper

1. Preheat the oven to 190°C/375°F/gas 5. Butter six ramekin dishes and put in a roasting or baking tin.

2. Cook the carrots and onion in the butter in a saucepan for about 5 minutes.

5. Add vegetable stock or water to cover the vegetables and simmer, uncovered, until the vegetables are tender and the liquid has evaporated.

4. Transfer the carrot mixture to a blender, add the eggs, crème fraîche and lemon juice and process until smooth. Add the parsley and seasoning and divide between the ramekin dishes. Pour boiling water around the dishes and cook in the oven for 20–25 minutes until just set in the centre.

5. To make the sauce melt the butter but do not allow to become too hot.

6. Put the egg yolks and lemon juice in a blender or food processor and mix briefly. With the motor running slowly pour in the melted butter to make a sauce with the consistency of double cream. Add the ginger and seasoning.

7. Leave the timbales to stand for a few minutes before unmoulding on to warm plates. Spoon some of the sauce over them and some around. Serve immediately.

CHAPTER TWO

Fish & Shellfish

Fish is ideal for the cook in a hurry because it cooks quickly. The speed at which it cooks depends on the type and texture of the fish (the softer the flesh, the quicker it cooks, so plaice cooks more quickly than monkfish or tuna); its temperature; the thickness of the piece or the whole fish (thin pieces and thin-bodied fish take proportionately less time to cook than thick ones); whether it has been marinated, and for how long (acid ingredients, such as citrus juices, vinegars and wines, 'cook' fish so the longer it is marinated, the softer it will become).

With the exception of very oily fish, such as mackerel, it is better to undercook fish than to overcook it, and some fish, such as salmon and tuna, are often cooked so that they are slightly 'rare' in the centre. Don't forget that the flesh will continue to cook if the fish is kept warm before serving. Creamy white beads of curd in the spaces between the flakes of fish are an indication that the fish is cooked. Alternatively, you can tell if the fish is ready by inserting the point of a sharp knife or a skewer in the thickest part or alongside the bone, if present, and if the flesh parts easily, it is cooked.

Quite a number of supermarkets now have wet fish counters that stock a good variety of fish. All the fish used in this book can be bought from a supermarket fish counter, although I have managed to find a very good fishmonger. He may not have as many of the exotic varieties as the larger supermarkets but he personally buys much of his fish fresh every day so I know it will be fresh rather than frozen. Remember that just because fish on a supermarket slab is not frozen when you see it, it does not mean that it has never been frozen. The fishmonger's crab will have been freshly cooked by him in the morning, as will many of his prawns. Catches do, of course, vary and I always telephone him a day or so in advance to check that he is likely to get what I want; if he can't get, for example, crab or scallops, I choose a different dish rather than use frozen. Fish should be bought on the day of the dinner party and kept cool in between buying and cooking.

TUNA WITH MINT VINAIGRETTE

·

SERVES 4

THIS is a very useful recipe because not only is it very quick and easy to make and cook, but it lends itself to simple changes of face. For example, basil can be used instead of mint, and salmon or red mullet instead of tuna. If the fish is very thin, grill it on one side only.

4 fresh tuna steaks, each weighing about 175g (6oz)
115ml (4fl oz) virgin olive oil
2½ tablespoons chopped mint
6 well-flavoured tomatoes
2 shallots

1 garlic clove
1 tablespoon chopped parsley
1 tablespoon lime juice
1 tablespoon white wine vinegar
salt and freshly ground black pepper
mint sprigs for garnish

1. Brush the tuna with 2 tablespoons of the oil, then sprinkle over 1 tablespoon of the mint, and pepper to taste. Set aside for as long as possible (up to 2 hours).

2. Meanwhile, peel, seed and chop the tomatoes, finely chop the shallots, and crush the garlic. Put the remaining oil and remaining ingredients, except the mint sprigs, in a screw-top jar and shake together. Add the tomato, shallots and garlic.

3. Preheat the grill.

4. Grill the tuna for 3–3½ minutes on each side until cooked but still pink in the centre.

5. Spoon the mint dressing on to four plates, and put a tuna steak on top. Garnish with mint sprigs.

BASS WITH GINGER VINAIGRETTE

·

THE vinaigrette can be made in advance; in fact the flavour will improve if it has some time (even 15–30 minutes) to develop, but do not add the coriander until just before serving as it will darken. Other fish, such as red snapper, salmon or tuna, can be used instead of sea bass.

·

6 sea bass fillets, each weighing about 175g (6oz)
olive oil for brushing
salt and freshly ground black pepper
toasted sesame seeds for garnish

VINAIGRETTE
1 red onion, finely chopped
50ml (2fl oz) rice vinegar

2.5cm (1 inch) piece of fresh root ginger, grated
juice of 2 limes
2 tablespoons soy sauce
225ml (8fl oz) virgin olive oil
2 tablespoons dark sesame oil
leaves from a bunch of coriander
salt and freshly ground black pepper

·

1. Preheat the grill. Put all the vinaigrette ingredients, except the coriander, in a screw-top jar and shake together vigorously until well emulsified.

2. Brush both sides of the sea bass with a little oil and grill for 1–2 minutes on each side, depending on the thickness. Do not overcook the fish.

3. Meanwhile, reserve a few of the coriander leaves for garnish and chop the remainder. Add to the vinaigrette, with seasoning, then pour a pool on to each of four plates.

4. Season the fish and place on the vinaigrette. Garnish with sesame seeds and the reserved coriander leaves.

SWORDFISH WITH PIQUANT BUTTER

•

— SERVES 6 —

SWORDFISH can be a little dry, but here the butter lubricates it, and the piquancy makes a good contrast to the meatiness of the flesh.

6 swordfish steaks, each weighing about 175g (6oz)
1 small lemon, halved
melted butter for brushing
salt and freshly ground black pepper

PIQUANT BUTTER
1 shallot, finely chopped
1 plump garlic clove, finely crushed
1½ tablespoons finely chopped parsley

1½ tablespoons finely chopped gherkins
1½ tablespoons finely chopped capers
4 drops of Worcestershire sauce
3–4 drops of Tabasco sauce
130g (4½oz) unsalted butter, at room temperature
salt and freshly ground black pepper (optional)

1. Make the piquant butter by beating the shallot, garlic, parsley, gherkins, capers, Worcestershire sauce and Tabasco sauce into the butter. Season lightly if liked. Form into a fat roll, wrap in cling film and freeze for about 20 minutes.

2. Preheat the grill. Squeeze lemon juice over the swordfish, season and brush both sides with melted butter. Grill for 5 minutes on each side, squeezing over more lemon juice and brushing with butter when turning the steaks.

3. Transfer the steaks to a warm serving plate and keep warm.

4. Unwrap the piquant butter and cut into six slices. Top each swordfish steak with a piece of butter and serve straight away.

OPPOSITE: Spice-Encrusted Prawns (page 43), Couscous (page 95) and Baked Baby Aubergines (page 90)

GRILLED SALMON STEAKS WITH TOMATOES AND BASIL

·

— SERVES 6 —

SALMON, herbs and tomatoes are at their best in the summer, so that is when I usually serve what is one of my favourite main courses, although it can be served at other times of the year.

6 salmon steaks, each weighing about 175g (6oz)
8 tablespoons virgin olive oil, plus extra olive oil for brushing
3 tablespoons balsamic vinegar

50g (2oz) basil
12 well-flavoured tomatoes
$2\frac{1}{2}$ tablespoons chopped tarragon
salt and freshly ground black pepper

1. Brush the salmon with olive oil and vinegar. Season and leave for 30 minutes.

2. Meanwhile, mix the virgin olive oil and basil together in a small blender or food processor. Set aside.

3. Finely chop the tomatoes and mix with the tarragon and seasoning.

4. Preheat the grill. Grill the salmon for about 4 minutes on each side or until just cooked through.

5. Divide the tomatoes and tarragon between six plates. Put a salmon steak on top, trickle over the basil oil, and serve.

OPPOSITE: Mediterranean Fish Casserole (page 45)

CRISP-TOPPED BAKED SALMON FILLET

·

—— SERVES 6 ——

As the skin is left on the fish, make sure the scales have been removed. (The fishmonger should do this.) The skin is scored into a diamond pattern to help the fish cook quickly and evenly; it also, incidentally, means that guests are not confronted by large pieces of fish skin, which some find off-putting.

900g (2lb) salmon fillet
125g (4½ oz) ciabatta
2 large shallots, chopped
2 garlic cloves
40g (1½ oz) pitted black olives
20g (¾ oz) anchovy fillets
1 tablespoon basil

1½ tablespoons virgin olive oil, plus extra
   for trickling
salt and freshly ground black pepper
Red Pepper and Tomato Sauce (see page
   96) or Tomato and Red Pepper Salsa
   (see page 100) to serve

1. Preheat the oven to 230°C/450°F/gas 8. Using a sharp knife, slash the skin side of the salmon in parallel lines, first in one direction and then in the other, at right angles to the first, to make a diamond pattern.

2. Break the ciabatta into pieces and drop into a blender or food processor. Add the shallots, garlic, black olives, anchovies, basil and seasoning and mix to coarse crumbs. Stir in the 1½ tablespoons oil.

3. Press the crumb mixture into the skin side of the salmon and put in a shallow baking dish. Trickle olive oil over and bake for 10–15 minutes or until brown and crisp on the outside and just cooked on the inside.

SALMON FILLET WITH TOMATO AND SOY SAUCE

·

Soy sauce adds depth to this tomato sauce, and the butter that is swirled in just before serving gives it a sheen. Serve with mashed or new potatoes and a green vegetable such as French beans, mangetout, asparagus or broccoli.

·

50g (2oz) unsalted butter, diced	1 large well-flavoured tomato, deseeded
115g (4oz) shallots, finely chopped	and diced
300ml ($\frac{1}{2}$ pint) fish stock	4 tablespoons soy sauce
675g (1$\frac{1}{2}$lb) salmon fillet	freshly ground black pepper

·

1. Heat the butter in a frying pan, add the shallots and fry until very soft. Add the stock and bring to the boil, then simmer until reduced by half.

2. Meanwhile, skin the salmon. Beat the salmon lightly with a rolling pin to flatten it slightly, then cut across into 2.5cm (1 inch) strips. Season with pepper.

3. Heat a non-stick frying pan, add the salmon and fry quickly for about 30 seconds on each side. Remove to a warm plate and keep warm.

4. Add any salmon juices, the tomato and soy sauce to the stock and boil until reduced a little further. Gradually swirl in the remaining butter, making sure each piece is incorporated before adding the next.

5. Divide the fish and sauce between four warm plates.

SALMON STEAKS WITH SUN-DRIED TOMATO AND OLIVE BUTTER

·

—— SERVES 6 ——

DEPENDING on which is more convenient, the salmon, which is enclosed in parcels, can be steamed or baked.

6 salmon steaks, each weighing about
   150g (5oz)
juice of $\frac{1}{2}$–1 lemon
salt and freshly ground black pepper
6 basil sprigs for garnish
lemon wedges to serve

SUN-DRIED TOMATO AND OLIVE
   BUTTER
115g (4oz) unsalted butter, softened
1 small garlic clove
$\frac{1}{2}$ small bunch of chives
15g ($\frac{1}{2}$oz) black olives, pitted
1$\frac{1}{2}$ tablespoons sun-dried tomato paste

1. Bring a saucepan of water to the boil or preheat the oven to 200°C/400°F/gas 6. Put the ingredients for the sun–dried tomato and olive butter into a blender or food processor and mix until smooth.

2. Brush the salmon with lemon juice, season and put each steak on a piece of greaseproof paper or foil large enough to enclose it. Divide the butter between the steaks, then fold the paper or foil loosely around the fish and secure the edges tightly. Steam or bake for about 15 minutes.

3. Open the parcels slightly and garnish each piece of fish with basil. Serve with lemon wedges.

BABY SALMON WITH FENNEL MAYONNAISE

•

— SERVES 6 —

GONE are the days when the only time most of us could justify serving a whole salmon was when catering for a large number. Now, young salmon (also known as grilse), weighing from 1.35–1.8kg (3–4lb) and ideal for 4–6 people, are being sold by supermarkets and some fishmongers. Golden Potatoes (see page 86) make a fitting accompaniment. Instead of the fennel mayonnaise, a yogurt and cucumber salad, flavoured with either dill or mint (see page 91), can be served. Alternatively, make double the quantity of Olive Oil Hollandaise Sauce (see page 89).

1.8kg (4lb) salmon
150ml (5fl oz) medium-bodied dry white
  wine
a few fennel sprigs
1 bay leaf, torn
salt and freshly ground black pepper
fennel sprigs for garnish

FENNEL MAYONNAISE
1 fennel bulb
2 garlic cloves, crushed and thinly sliced
350ml (12fl oz) mayonnaise, preferably
  home-made
4–5 tablespoons chopped fennel
about 1 tablespoon Pernod

---

1. Preheat the oven to 180°C/350°F/gas 4. Lay the fish on a sheet of oiled foil on a baking sheet, sprinkle over the wine, scatter the fennel and bay leaf over the top and add the seasoning. Fold the foil over loosely and twist the edges together firmly to seal tightly. Bake for about 35 minutes or until the salmon flesh flakes easily when tested with the point of a sharp knife.

2. Meanwhile, bring a saucepan of water to the boil while chopping the fennel bulb finely. Add the fennel to the water and blanch for 1 minute. Tip into a colander, then rinse under running cold water. Drain well, then tip on to several thicknesses of absorbent kitchen paper to dry.

3. Stir the blanched fennel and garlic into the mayonnaise, then add chopped fennel and Pernod to taste.

4. Carefully transfer the salmon to a warmed serving plate and garnish with fennel sprigs. Serve the fennel mayonnaise separately.

RED MULLET WITH GINGER AND TOMATO

•

—— SERVES 4 ——

For some reason it surprises me that tomatoes and ginger go together, but they do go together well, and the combination complements the flavour of red mullet. This recipe looks far more complicated and time-consuming than it is. The fish can be grilled while the sauce is being made, and the whole dish should be ready in less than 10 minutes.

1½ tablespoons groundnut oil

2 shallots, chopped

1 fresh red chilli, deseeded and finely chopped

4 garlic cloves, crushed

50g (2oz) piece of fresh root ginger

8 well-flavoured tomatoes, deseeded and quite finely chopped

150ml (5fl oz) fish stock

2 spring onions

leaves from a sprig of coriander

50g (2oz) unsalted butter, diced

2 red mullet, each weighing about 400g (14oz), filleted

salt

lemon wedges to serve

1. Heat the oil in a frying pan, add the shallots, chilli and garlic, and fry for 2 minutes. Preheat the grill.

2. Meanwhile, grate the ginger and add to the pan while the ingredients are frying.

3. Add the tomatoes and stock, bring quickly to the boil, and then simmer for 2 minutes.

4. While the sauce is simmering, chop the white part of the spring onions, and the coriander.

5. Gradually swirl the butter into the sauce, making sure each piece is incorporated before adding the next. Add the spring onions and coriander, and season with salt.

6. While the sauce is cooking, very lightly brush the fish fillets with oil, then grill, skin-side up, for about 5 minutes.

7. Pour the sauce on to four warmed plates and put a piece of fish on top. Add a lemon wedge and serve.

ROAST MONKFISH WITH PARMA HAM

·

—— SERVES 4 ——

MAKE sure all the fine membrane is removed from the monkfish because it shrinks when cooked and distorts the monkfish. I try to prepare the fish about 1 hour in advance so the flavours have time to mellow before cooking. I usually serve the monkfish with steamed spinach.

Tapenade with Sun-dried Tomatoes (see page 97), Pesto (see page 98) or Red Pepper Pesto (see page 99) for spreading
700g (1½lb) monkfish tail, filleted
6 slices of Parma ham

SAUCE (optional)
550g (1¼lb) well-flavoured tomatoes
2 shallots

3 tablespoons crème fraîche or soured cream
3 tablespoons balsamic vinegar
1½ teaspoons dry sherry
¾ teaspoon Dijon mustard
2 teaspoons chopped parsley
salt and freshly ground black pepper

1. Preheat the oven to 200°C/400°F/gas 6. Spread the chosen pesto or tapenade over the inside of the monkfish fillets, put them back together and wrap in the Parma ham so the fish is completely covered. Tie the Parma ham in place. Place in a roasting tin, brush with oil and bake in the oven for 15–20 minutes or until the fish is opaque.

2. Meanwhile, make the sauce, if liked. Halve the tomatoes and remove the seeds and juice (they can be used in cooked tomato sauce or in casseroles). Reserve two tomato halves and put the remainder in a blender. Chop the shallots and put about three-quarters into the blender. Add the crème fraîche or soured cream, vinegar, sherry and mustard, and mix to a purée. Chop the reserved tomato, finely chop the reserved shallot and add both to the sauce with the parsley and seasoning.

3. Serve the monkfish sliced, and accompanied by the sauce, if using.

CRISP MONKFISH PACKAGES

·

—— SERVES 6 ——

INSIDE its crisp filo pastry package, the monkfish has a surprise topping of a savoury cheese and rocket spread. To make the recipe even simpler, you could use Pesto (see page 98), Red Pepper Pesto (see page 99), Salsa Verde (see page 87) or Tapenade with Sun-dried Tomatoes (see page 97) instead of the rocket spread.

50g (2oz) ricotta cheese
50g (2oz) rocket
2 tablespoons chopped parsley
1 garlic clove
1 tablespoon walnut pieces
25g (1oz) freshly grated Parmesan cheese, plus extra for sprinkling
grated zest and juice of $\frac{1}{2}$ lime

2 tablespoons olive oil, plus extra for brushing
3 sheets of filo pastry, each about 30 × 20cm (12 × 8 inches)
6 thick monkfish fillets, each weighing about 115g (4oz)
salt and freshly ground black pepper
beaten egg for brushing

1. Preheat the oven to 200°C/400°F/gas 6.

2. Put the cheese, rocket, parsley, garlic, walnuts, Parmesan, lime zest and juice, and 2 tablespoons olive oil in a blender and mix until smooth. Season to taste.

3. Cut 12 pieces of filo pastry, each large enough to enclose a piece of fish. Brush one piece with oil, cover with another piece, then put a piece of fish in the centre. Spread with one-sixth of the rocket mixture. Fold over the pastry to enclose the fish, and press the edges together to seal. Put on a greased baking sheet, seam-side down. Repeat with the remaining pastry, fish and rocket mixture.

4. Brush all the parcels with oil, then bake in the oven for 10 minutes. Brush the tops with beaten egg and sprinkle with grated Parmesan, then bake for about another 8 minutes or until golden.

RED SNAPPER WITH PROVENÇAL SALSA

•

—— SERVES 4 ——

RED snapper is the finest of the snapper family for eating, having firm, savoury white flesh. Orange roughy and mahi mahi (also known as dolphin fish), two other 'exotic' fish from the Pacific which have begun appearing in supermarkets and fishmongers, are also suitable and make a talking point. Alternatively, you could use cod (make sure it is really fresh) or monkfish. The salsa can be made in advance and kept in a covered container in the refrigerator.

•

4 large red snapper fillets
1 tablespoon thyme
1 tablespoon balsamic vinegar
3 tablespoons olive oil

SALSA
1 large red onion, finely chopped
5 plum tomatoes, finely chopped
115g (4oz) mixed pitted black and green
  olives, finely chopped

2 tablespoons chopped parsley
3 tablespoons capers
1 teaspoon chilli paste
1 tablespoon white wine vinegar
1 tablespoon balsamic vinegar
2 tablespoons virgin olive oil
salt and freshly ground black pepper

•

1. Put the snapper fillets in a shallow non-metallic dish. Sprinkle over the thyme and pour over the vinegar and oil. Turn the fillets over, cover and marinate for 1–2 hours or overnight.

2. To make the salsa, mix all the ingredients together.

3. Preheat the grill. Remove the fish from the marinade, reserving the marinade. Grill for 4–5 minutes or until the flesh just flakes, brushing once or twice with the marinade. Serve with the salsa.

PROVENÇAL BRILL FILLET ROLLS

·

—— SERVES 4 ——

I KNOW brill is not a Provençal fish, but it makes an effective marriage with Provençal ingredients in this simple yet well-flavoured dish.

4 brill fillets, each weighing about 175g (6oz)
2 tablespoons black olive paste
juice of 1 large lemon
2 well-flavoured tomatoes

2 tablespoons pitted black olives
2 tablespoons capers
2 tablespoons chopped parsley
freshly ground black pepper

1. Preheat the grill. Skin the fillets and cut in half lengthways. Spread a little black olive paste over each strip, then roll up and put, seam-side down, in the grill pan. Squeeze over the lemon juice and season with black pepper. Grill for 4–5 minutes.

2. Meanwhile, chop the tomatoes, discarding the seeds if liked. Chop the black olives and mix with the tomatoes, capers, parsley and black pepper.

3. Serve the fish rolls with the tomato mixture.

BRILL WITH FRAGRANT COCONUT SAUCE

•

—— SERVES 6 ——

THIS very quick dish is elegant, delicate and light. Brill is a highly regarded fish with a fine, sweet flavour and creamy, slightly firm flesh. It belongs to the same family as turbot and although it does not quite compare to turbot's excellence, it is cheaper so offers better value. Couscous, with butter (see page 95), Golden Potatoes (see page 86) or wide ribbon pasta are fitting accompaniments. If the whole meal is to be light, Cherry Compote (see page 119) would be a suitable dessert, but if you would like to serve something more substantial, try Plum Tart (see page 107), Soft Fruit Tart (see page 108) or Apricot and Amaretti Crumble (see page 109).

•

25g (1oz) unsalted butter, diced

1 onion, finely chopped

$1\frac{1}{2}$ stalks of lemon grass

2 tablespoons lime juice

4cm ($1\frac{1}{2}$ inch) piece of fresh root ginger, grated

$2\frac{1}{2}$ teaspoons Thai fish sauce (nam pla)

425ml (15fl oz) coconut milk

6 brill fillets, each weighing about 175g (6oz)

finely grated zest of $1\frac{1}{2}$ limes

3–4 tablespoons chopped coriander

freshly ground black pepper

sprigs of coriander for garnish

•

1. Heat the butter in a wide frying pan, add the onion and cook until softened but not coloured.

2. Meanwhile, slice the lemon grass lengthways and finely chop. Mix with the lime juice, ginger, fish sauce, coconut milk and pepper. Pour into the pan and heat gently.

3. Halve each brill fillet lengthways, and fold in half across the middle. Add to the sauce and spoon some of the sauce over the fish. Cover and poach for 4–5 minutes or until the flesh just flakes.

4. Using a slotted spoon, transfer the fish to a warmed serving plate. Cover and keep warm. Add the coriander to the sauce and boil to thicken it slightly. Adjust the seasoning, then pour over the fish and garnish with the lime zest and a few coriander leaves.

SPICE-TOPPED FISH WITH RED PEPPER SAUCE

•

SERVES 6

ALTHOUGH the whole dish can be prepared and cooked quickly, to give you less to do on the evening of the dinner party, and to speed things along slightly, the red pepper sauce and the topping can be made in advance, even in the morning before going to work.

•

3 red peppers

$1\frac{1}{2}$ tablespoons virgin olive oil

$1\frac{1}{2}$ teaspoons balsamic vinegar

6 tuna or salmon steaks, each weighing about 175g (6oz)

salt and freshly ground black pepper

TOPPING

1 large red onion, coarsely chopped

3 garlic cloves

$4\frac{1}{2}$ tablespoons chopped parsley

$4\frac{1}{2}$ tablespoons chopped coriander

3 teaspoons ground cumin

3 tablespoons mild chilli powder

4 tablespoons olive oil

$1\frac{1}{2}$ tablespoons lime juice

salt and freshly ground black pepper

•

1. Preheat the grill. Cut the peppers in half, then grill until charred and blistered. Leave until cool enough to handle, then remove the skins, seeds and cores. Purée the pepper flesh with the oil and vinegar in a blender or food processor. Season to taste.

2. Mix all the ingredients for the topping in a blender or food processor until reduced to a paste. Spread half firmly over one side of each piece of fish.

3. Grill the fish on an oiled rack, topping side up, for about 4 minutes or until the topping is beginning to blacken. Carefully turn the fish over, spread with the remaining topping and grill for a further 4 minutes.

4. Serve the fish with the red pepper sauce.

SPICE-ENCRUSTED PRAWNS

•

— SERVES 4 —

THE fragrant but not hot spice mixture clings to the prawns in this simple dish. Sesame and Coriander Noodles (see page 94), or Couscous, with butter (see page 95) are suitable accompaniments.

1½ stalks of lemon grass, halved lengthways and chopped

7.5cm (3 inch) piece of fresh root ginger, coarsely chopped

½ large red pepper, deseeded and coarsely chopped

½ teaspoon cayenne pepper or 1 fresh red chilli, deseeded

4 garlic cloves

1½ tablespoons sliced almonds

3 shallots, chopped

¾ teaspoon ground turmeric

1 tablespoon lime juice

5 tablespoons groundnut oil

salt

700g (1½lb) peeled raw king prawns

1. Put all the ingredients, except the oil and prawns, into a small blender with about 6 tablespoons water, and mix to a smooth paste.

2. Heat the oil in a frying pan (preferably non-stick), over a medium heat until very hot. Add the spice paste and fry, stirring frequently, until reduced and darkened to reddish brown. Stir in the prawns and fry over a high heat for 4–5 minutes or until the prawns are just cooked and the paste thickened and clinging to the prawns.

3. Using a slotted spoon, transfer the prawns to warm serving plates, leaving the oil in the pan.

SAFFRON SCALLOPS

•

— SERVES 6 —

As this is a very special dish, do try to use fresh rather than frozen scallops as they will make all the difference. The dill garnish does more than just make the dish look pretty; it also adds to the wonderful overall blend of flavours. Serve with lightly cooked spinach tossed in lemon juice.

•

50g (2oz) unsalted butter, diced
900g (2lb) shelled fresh scallops
2 large shallots, finely chopped
1 garlic clove, crushed
175ml (6fl oz) dry white vermouth

pinch of saffron strands, crushed
300ml ($\frac{1}{2}$ pint) crème fraîche
salt and freshly ground white or black
 pepper
dill sprigs for garnish

•

1. Heat half the butter in a large non-stick frying pan. Add the scallops in batches so they are not crowded in the pan, and fry quickly for 1–2 minutes or until golden on the outside and only just tender in the centre. Set aside.

2. Add the remaining butter to the pan, heat through, then add the shallots and garlic. Cook until softened, then add the vermouth, saffron strands and crème fraîche. Bubble for 4–5 minutes or until reduced and syrupy. Season.

3. Return the scallops to the pan. Heat through gently for 1–2 minutes, then serve garnished with dill.

MEDITERRANEAN FISH CASSEROLE

·

THE selection of fish and shellfish can be changed according to your taste – for example, mussels could be added. Serve with good ciabatta or focaccia bread to soak up the juices.

·

2 tablespoons olive oil

3 red onions, thinly sliced

3 garlic cloves, crushed

3 red peppers

$\frac{3}{4}$ teaspoon paprika pepper

175ml (6fl oz) medium-bodied dry white wine

three 400g (14oz) cans of chopped tomatoes

$1\frac{1}{2}$ tablespoons sun-dried tomato paste

bouquet garni

900g (2lb) skinless firm white fish, such as monkfish, cod, halibut, haddock

175g (6oz) peeled large raw prawns, halved

175g (6oz) black olives, preferably oil-cured, pitted

salt and freshly ground black pepper

basil, thyme or parsley for garnish

·

1. Heat the oil in a flameproof casserole, add the onions and garlic, and fry until softened but not coloured.

2. Meanwhile, deseed and thinly slice the peppers.

3. Stir the peppers into the casserole, then sprinkle over the paprika and stir for 1 minute. Add the wine, and boil until reduced by half.

4. Add the tomatoes, sun-dried tomato paste, bouquet garni and seasoning, bring to the boil, then simmer, uncovered, for 15 minutes, stirring occasionally.

5. While the casserole is simmering, cut the fish in 2.5–4cm (1–1$\frac{1}{2}$ inch) pieces.

6. Add the fish and prawns to the casserole, and continue to simmer for 3–5 minutes or until they are just cooked. Stir in the olives. Serve garnished with basil, thyme or parsley.

— CHAPTER THREE —

Poultry & Game

POULTRY or, more specifically, chicken, is the most popular and acceptable meat in Britain; some people who will not eat any other meat will eat poultry. Because it is so widely acceptable, it is a good, safe choice for a dinner party, but on the other hand you might feel that it is too 'ordinary'. To overcome this, buy a really good, fresh, free-range bird. It will not have the flabby, tasteless flesh so often associated with chicken, but will be a real treat with flavoursome, firm flesh. To tell whether chicken is cooked through, which it must be before it is served, pierce the thickest part, next to the bone if appropriate, with a fine, sharp knife. If the juices run clear, the flesh is done; if the juices are still pink, cook the chicken for a little longer.

Duck used to be a very fatty meat and this, together with the fact that a duck has a high ratio of bone to flesh, meant that it was an uneconomical buy. Now, through selective breeding, duck are leaner and new, better-flavoured varieties, such as Barbary, have been introduced. Duck breasts are sold off the bone to save wastage, and are quick to cook. Duck is often cooked until it is slightly pink, and should never be overcooked.

Feathered game is one food that remains seasonal and in limited supply (although it is more generally available with many supermarkets selling it) so is always something of a treat and so suitable for a dinner party. I prefer partridge to pheasant because the flavour is more subtle and complex and the flesh more tender. They are not as plentiful as pheasant, which makes them more special, and they are small enough to roast in about 30 minutes. The partridge season starts on 1 September, but many shoots do not begin until at least a month or so later, even into November when pheasant shooting begins in earnest. The season ends on 1 February but birds shot in the new year are larger and tougher so are not so suitable for plain roasting. I always buy game birds from a butcher/game dealer; those from a supermarket seem to lack character.

Thanks to deer farming, venison is now quite widely available, but it is still eaten sufficiently infrequently by most people to make it a treat. As it is one of the most healthy meats, you will also be doing your guests a favour.

ITALIAN ROAST CHICKEN AND VEGETABLES

•

—— SERVES 4–6 ——

THE vegetables and pancetta can be prepared while the oven is heating.

450g (1lb) courgettes, cut into wedges	6 boneless chicken breasts
450g (1lb) each red and yellow peppers, quartered	115g (4oz) pancetta, finely chopped
2 garlic cloves	225ml (8fl oz) medium-bodied dry white wine
115g (4oz) pitted oil-cured black olives	225ml (8fl oz) chicken stock
2 tablespoons capers	salt and freshly ground black pepper
3 tablespoons finely chopped rosemary	
4 tablespoons olive oil	

1. Preheat the oven to 220°C/425°F/gas 7. Put the courgettes, peppers, garlic cloves, olives, capers and half the rosemary into a roasting tin. Season and pour over the oil. Roast in the oven for 15 minutes.

2. Lower the oven temperature to 200°C/400°F/gas 6. Put the chicken on top of the vegetables and scatter over the pancetta and remaining rosemary. Roast for a further 25 minutes.

3. Remove the chicken and vegetables to a warm serving dish, leaving the garlic behind. Keep the chicken warm.

4. Stir the wine into the roasting tin, mashing the garlic with a fork. Boil hard for 2–3 minutes, then add the stock and boil hard again until lightly thickened. Season and serve with the chicken and vegetables.

POACHED CHICKEN BREASTS WITH CORIANDER AND GINGER MAYONNAISE

·

—— SERVES 6 ——

THE chicken can also be served cold; after poaching, leave it to cool in the liquid so that the flesh stays succulent and tender.

150ml ($\frac{1}{4}$ pint) medium-bodied dry white wine (optional)

approximately 2.5cm (1 inch) piece of unpeeled fresh root ginger

bouquet garni

pared rind of 1 lime

6 boneless chicken breast fillets

coriander sprigs for garnish

CORIANDER AND GINGER MAYONNAISE

2 egg yolks

$\frac{3}{4}$ teaspoon Dijon mustard

1 garlic clove

about 1 teaspoon grated fresh root ginger

300ml ($\frac{1}{2}$ pint) mild olive oil

5 tablespoons Greek yogurt

juice of 1–1$\frac{1}{2}$ limes

4–5 tablespoons chopped coriander

salt and freshly ground black pepper

1. Fill a large frying pan with the wine, if used, and enough water to cover the chicken in a single layer. Crush the ginger with a rolling pin, then add to the water with the bouquet garni and lime rind. When the water boils, add the chicken and return to simmering point, then cover and cook gently for 20–25 minutes.

2. Meanwhile, make the mayonnaise. Put the egg yolks, mustard, garlic and 1 teaspoon grated ginger into a blender. Mix briefly, then, with the motor running, slowly pour in the oil until the sauce thickens. Add the yogurt, lime juice and coriander, and season to taste. Add more ginger if necessary.

3. Using a slotted spoon, transfer the chicken to warmed plates and garnish with coriander sprigs. Add a large spoonful of the mayonnaise to each plate and serve the rest separately.

ZIPPY ST CLEMENT'S CHICKEN

·

—— SERVES 6 ——

MILD spices and orange and lemon juices, lightly sweetened with a touch of honey, make this a light, elegant dish that won't break the bank.

½ teaspoon ground ginger
½ teaspoon ground cinnamon
2 garlic cloves, crushed
6 boneless chicken breasts
2 tablespoons olive oil
1 tablespoon grated fresh root ginger
1 tablespoon grated orange zest
juice of 2 oranges

1 teaspoon grated lemon zest
juice of 1 lemon
1 tablespoon clear honey
175ml (6fl oz) chicken stock
salt and freshly ground black pepper
coriander or parsley leaves or chopped
    chives for garnish

1. Mix together the ground ginger, cinnamon and garlic, and rub over the chicken.

2. Heat the oil in a large, heavy-based frying pan, add the chicken, skin-side down first, and brown the chicken on both sides.

3. Add the remaining ingredients, except the garnish, and bring to just on boiling point. Cover tightly and cook so the liquid is barely bubbling for about 20 minutes or until the chicken is cooked, turning the chicken several times.

4. Serve garnished with coriander or parsley leaves or chopped chives.

GRILLED CHICKEN WITH VERMOUTH AND LIME

.

—— SERVES 6 ——

VERMOUTHS are flavoured with a variety of herbs. Each brand has its own special blend, so they do vary in flavour, some being more herbal than others. The more pronounced the flavour of the vermouth, the more character it will add to this dish.

.

6 boneless chicken breasts with skin, each weighing about 175g (6oz)

7 tablespoons chopped coriander

finely grated zest and juice of 3 limes

4 tablespoons dry white vermouth

2 garlic cloves, crushed

75ml (3fl oz) virgin olive oil

salt and freshly ground black pepper

several spring onions, and lime wedges to serve

.

1. Put the chicken in a non-metallic dish. Mix together 5 tablespoons of the coriander, the lime and juice, vermouth, garlic, oil and black pepper, and pour over the chicken. Turn the chicken over, then leave for 30–60 minutes, if possible, turning the chicken over once.

2. Preheat the grill and line the grill pan with foil.

3. Grill the chicken for 10–12 minutes on each side, basting occasionally with the marinade.

4. Meanwhile, slice the spring onions diagonally and mix with the remaining coriander.

5. Transfer the chicken to warm plates. Sprinkle with salt then spoon over any remaining marinade and sprinkle with the spring onion and coriander mixture. Serve with lime wedges.

BAKED SESAME CHICKEN

·

—— SERVES 6 ——

WITH a good chicken, roast chicken is one of my favourite meats, but it is not possible in 30 minutes or so. This recipe, however, is a good substitute. The crisp coating keeps the flesh succulent during baking, and provides an interesting texture and flavour when you are eating the chicken.

6 skinless, boneless chicken breasts
about 7g (¼oz) unsalted butter
4 tablespoons sesame oil
5 tablespoons seasoned flour
2–3 large eggs, beaten
6 tablespoons fresh breadcrumbs
6 tablespoons sesame seeds

lime slices and coriander sprigs for garnish

MARINADE
1 tablespoon soy sauce
juice of 3 limes
1 tablespoon chopped coriander

1. Mix the marinade ingredients together and pour over the chicken. Leave to marinate for at least 15 minutes, turning the chicken a couple of times.

2. Preheat the oven to 200°C/400°F/gas 6. Put the butter and sesame oil in a shallow roasting tin and heat in the oven for about 10 minutes.

3. Remove the chicken from the marinade and pat dry. Coat evenly and lightly with the seasoned flour, and pat the flour gently into the chicken. Dip in beaten egg, allowing the excess to flow off. Mix together the breadcrumbs and sesame seeds, then coat the chicken in the mixture, pressing it in.

4. Put the chicken in the roasting tin, baste with the hot oil and butter, and bake for about 15 minutes, basting occasionally, until the chicken is crisp and brown and the juices run clear when a skewer is inserted into the thickest part of the flesh.

5. Serve garnished with lime slices and coriander sprigs.

BAKED CHICKEN IN COCONUT SAUCE

•

SERVES 6

IF you do not have any roasted spice seeds ready, and don't feel you have time to do them (it only takes a couple of minutes, though), use ground spices. Lightly spiced rice or Couscous (see page 95) is a good accompaniment.

1 garlic clove, crushed	2 onions grated
1 lemon grass stalk, halved lengthways and finely chopped	570ml (1 pint) coconut milk
	6 boneless chicken breasts
1 teaspoon each of finely crushed cumin seeds, finely crushed roasted coriander, mild chilli powder and ground turmeric	salt and freshly ground black pepper
	coriander sprigs for garnish
	lemon or lime wedges to serve

1. Preheat the oven to 200°C/400°F/gas 6. Mix together the garlic, lemon grass, spices, salt, onion and enough of the coconut milk to make a thick paste.

2. Put the chicken in a roasting tin and coat with the spice mixture. Pour the remaining coconut milk round the chicken and bake in the oven for 25 minutes, basting occasionally with the coconut milk.

3. Transfer the chicken to a warm serving plate and keep warm. Boil the coconut milk until very lightly thickened, and season to taste. Garnish the chicken with coriander, and serve with the coconut milk sauce and lemon or lime wedges.

FRAGRANT CHICKEN

·

—— SERVES 6 ——

ENTICING aromas herald the approach of succulent chunks of chicken bathed in a creamy, spiced coconut sauce. Jasmine rice, or Thai fragrant rice as it is sometimes known, is the most fitting accompaniment for soaking up the flavourful juices. Please do not be put off by the length of the ingredients list – everything is easy to buy and needs virtually no preparation.

1 onion, quartered

2 garlic cloves

1 red chilli

3cm ($1\frac{1}{4}$ inch) piece of fresh root ginger, halved

small handful of coriander leaves and fine stems

2 lemon grass stalks, halved

grated zest and juice of 1 lime

1 teaspoon ground coriander

2 tablespoons olive oil

6 chicken breast fillets, each cut into 3 pieces

2 large well-flavoured tomatoes

900ml ($1\frac{1}{2}$ pints) thick coconut milk

2 tablespoons Thai fish sauce (nam pla)

salt and freshly ground black pepper

coriander sprigs for garnish

lime wedges to serve

1. Put the onion, garlic, chilli, ginger, coriander, lemon grass, lime zest and juice, and ground coriander in a blender or small food processor and mix to a nubbly paste, adding 1–2 tablespoons water if necessary.

2. Heat the oil in a large heavy-based frying pan (preferably non-stick), add the spice mixture and cook over a fairly high heat for about 3 minutes, stirring constantly.

3. Stir in the chicken to coat with the spice mixture, and cook for about 5 minutes, stirring occasionally.

4. Meanwhile, peel, seed and chop the tomatoes and add to the pan with the coconut milk and fish sauce. Bring to just on simmering point, then cover the pan and cook very gently, stirring occasionally, for 20–25 minutes or until the chicken is tender.

5. Season if necessary (the fish sauce may provide enough salt). Serve garnished with coriander sprigs and accompanied by lime wedges.

CHICKEN AND AVOCADO STROGANOFF WITH PESTO

·

—— SERVES 6 ——

IF you make your own pesto, so much the better, but you can use a ready-prepared variety. Brands vary in quality so it is worth trying a number until you find the one you like. Adjust the amount you add to the sauce according to taste.

1 tablespoon olive oil
5 spring onions, sliced
6 skinless chicken breast fillets, total
  weight 600–675g (1¼–1½lb)
2 avocados
150ml (5fl oz) crème fraîche

175–225ml (6–8fl oz) pesto
salt and freshly ground black pepper
about 600g (1¼lb) tagliatelli or fettucine,
  boiled and drained, to serve
basil leaves for garnish

1. Heat the oil in a frying pan, add the spring onions and fry until softened but not coloured.

2. Meanwhile, cut the chicken into strips.

3. Add the chicken to the pan, and fry, turning as necessary, until cooked through.

4. While the chicken is cooking, halve, stone and peel the avocados and cut into thin strips.

5. Stir the crème fraîche and pesto into the chicken, then add the avocado and seasonings and heat through.

6. Serve the chicken mixture over the pasta and garnish with basil leaves.

TURKEY ROLLS WITH PESTO AND MOZZARELLA CHEESE

·

—— SERVES 6 ——

YOU might find one egg is enough for coating the rolls so start by beating just one, and then beating the other one if it is needed. Olive oil is less readily absorbed than other oils when frying foods, especially if it is correctly heated before the food is added.

6 turkey slices (escalopes), each weighing about 100g (3½oz)
1 plump garlic clove, finely crushed
4½ tablespoons pesto
75g (3oz) mozzarella cheese
1–2 eggs, beaten

about 150g (5oz) coarse polenta or dried breadcrumbs
olive oil for frying
salt and freshly ground black pepper
Red Pepper and Tomato Sauce (see page 96) to serve

1. Using a rolling pin, beat out each turkey slice between two sheets of greaseproof paper or clingfilm to make them thin and evenly flat. Spread with the garlic and pesto.

2. Cut the cheese into 12 fingers to fit almost the length of a turkey slice. Lay the cheese along the centre of the turkey, season and roll up to enclose the cheese completely.

3. Dip each roll in beaten egg and then in polenta or crumbs so the rolls are completely and evenly covered. Put in the freezer for 20 minutes.

4. Heat 1cm (½ inch) depth of olive oil until medium hot, then fry the rolls for 4–5 minutes on each side or until crisp and golden. Using a slotted spoon, transfer to absorbent kitchen paper to drain briefly. Serve straight away with Red Pepper and Tomato Sauce.

DUCK BREASTS WITH KUMQUATS

·

— SERVES 6 —

THE sharpness of the kumquats and the slightly spicy sweetness of the sauce marry well with the richness and flavour of duck breasts.

·

1 tablespoon olive oil
6 duck breasts, each weighing about 175g
  (6oz)
2 garlic cloves
350g (12oz) kumquats
1½ teaspoons ground cinnamon

4½ tablespoons clear honey
425ml (15fl oz) unsweetened apple juice
6 tablespoons lemon juice
1½ teaspoons balsamic or sherry vinegar
about 1 tablespoon caster sugar
salt and freshly ground black pepper

1. Heat the oil in a frying pan large enough to take the duck breasts in a single layer. Prick the skin of the breasts and add to the pan, skin-side down. Fry for 4 minutes on each side or until golden.

2. Meanwhile, lightly crush the garlic and slice the kumquats. Add the garlic to the duck about 2 minutes before the end of the cooking.

3. Stir the cinnamon, honey, apple juice, lemon juice, seasoning and 200ml (7fl oz) water into the pan. Add the kumquats and bring to the boil. Cover and simmer for about 15 minutes or until the duck is tender but still slightly pink inside.

4. Using a slotted fish slice or spoon, transfer the duck to a warm plate and keep warm. Stir the vinegar and sugar into the pan and boil for 2–3 minutes. Pour over the duck and serve.

BAKED DUCK BREASTS WITH TROPICAL SALSA

•

—— SERVES 6 ——

FRUIT is always popular with duck, and this salsa, with papaya and mango, gives an unusual, exotic twist to the theme. The salsa can be prepared in advance and kept in a covered container in the refrigerator. The duck can also be prepared in advance and left to marinate for 2–4 hours, if liked.

3 tablespoons dark soy sauce
1 tablespoon sesame oil
finely grated zest of 1 large orange
7.5cm (3 inch) piece of fresh root ginger, grated
1 tablespoon brown sugar
6 duck breasts, each weighing about 175g (6oz)

SALSA
1 ripe papaya, deseeded, peeled and chopped

1 small ripe mango, peeled, stoned and chopped
2–3 tablespoons lime juice
1 fresh red chilli, deseeded and finely chopped
1 red onion, finely chopped
leaves from a small bunch of coriander
salt and freshly ground black pepper

1. Preheat the oven to 230°C/450°F/gas 8. Mix together the soy sauce, sesame oil, orange zest, ginger and sugar. With the point of a sharp knife, cut several deep slashes in the duck skin. Repeat at 45° to the first cuts to make a diamond pattern. Put in a roasting or baking tin, pour over the soy mixture and turn the breasts over so both sides are coated. Leave skin-side up. Bake on the top shelf of the oven for 20 minutes or until the skin is crisp and brown and the flesh is pink.

2. Meanwhile, make the salsa by mixing all the ingredients together.

3. Serve the duck with the cooking juices spooned over and accompanied by the salsa.

GRILLED DUCK BREASTS WITH HONEY, SOY AND GINGER MARINADE

·

—— SERVES 6 ——

THIS really is a quick and easy dish to do for a dinner party because on the night there is no more to do than grill the breasts. It is also a good recipe to serve after a first course, or before a dessert, that requires quite a lot of attention.

·

6 duck breast fillets, each weighing about 175g (6oz)

MARINADE
1½ tablespoons clear honey
2 tablespoons light soy sauce
1½ tablespoons dark brown sugar
1½ tablespoons sesame oil

2 teaspoons wholegrain mustard
2 garlic cloves, finely crushed
finely grated zest of 1 small orange
1½ tablespoons red wine vinegar
4cm (1½ inch) piece of fresh root ginger, finely chopped
salt and freshly ground black pepper

·

1. Combine all the ingredients for the marinade.

2. Using a sharp knife, cut several deep slashes in the skin of each duck breast. Repeat at 45° to the first cuts to make a diamond pattern. Put in a shallow non-metallic dish and pour over the marinade. Turn the duck over and leave for as long as possible (up to 4–6 hours), turning occasionally.

3. Preheat the grill and oil the grill rack. Remove the breasts from the marinade, reserving the marinade. Grill the duck, skin-side first, for 12–15 minutes, turning occasionally and brushing with the marinade. The duck should be brown on the outside but still pink in the centre.

PARTRIDGE WITH MUSHROOMS

·

——— SERVES 4 ———

DEPENDING on where you buy the partridge, they may or may not have bacon over them. If they don't, put a slice over each breast to prevent the flesh becoming too dry.

4 slices of good streaky bacon (optional, see above)

4 partridge

6 thyme sprigs

1 garlic clove, lightly crushed

300g (10oz) wild or brown cap mushrooms, halved or quartered (according to size)

1 slice of good lightly smoked streaky bacon, finely chopped

1 bay leaf, torn

150g (5oz) medium-bodied red wine

75g (3oz) unsalted butter

salt and freshly ground black pepper

1. Preheat the oven to 220°C/425°F/gas 7. If necessary, tie a bacon slice over the breast of each partridge. Put a sprig of thyme in each bird and place in a roasting tin. Put the garlic, mushrooms, chopped bacon, remaining thyme and the bay leaf around the birds and pour over the wine. Put a knob of butter on each bird and dot the remainder over the mushrooms.

2. Roast the partridge for 20 minutes, basting with the cooking juices and stirring the mushrooms twice. Remove the bacon slices, baste and stir again, and roast for a further 5 minutes.

3. Transfer the partridge and mushrooms to a warm plate; use a slotted spoon to remove the mushrooms so the cooking juices are left behind. Boil the cooking juices until slightly syrupy. Season, pour over the partridge and serve.

VENISON WITH CRANBERRY AND APPLE RELISH

·

—— SERVES 6 ——

ALTHOUGH deer farming has made venison an easily obtainable meat, most people do not eat it very frequently, so it is a good choice for a dinner party. Venison is lean, so it is a healthy meat, but its leanness does mean that it should be marinated before cooking. Farmed venison has a milder flavour than wild venison; if you would like the venison to have a more distinctive flavour, leave it to marinate at room temperature (providing that is not too hot). Any relish that is left can be kept in a covered container in the fridge for up to 1 week, or even longer; it can be served hot or cold with pork or smoked venison or turkey, as well as with cooked venison or pheasant.

6 venison steaks, each weighing about 175g (6oz)
175ml (6fl oz) red wine
2 tablespoons olive oil
4 juniper berries, crushed
butter and oil for frying
salt and freshly ground black pepper

CRANBERRY AND APPLE RELISH
225g (8oz) fresh or frozen cranberries
about 300g (10oz) Bramley apple, peeled, cored and chopped
$\frac{1}{2}$ teaspoon mixed spice
115–175g (4–6oz) sugar
grated zest of 1 orange

1. Put the venison into a shallow non-metallic dish, add the wine, oil, juniper berries and pepper and turn the venison over. Cover and marinate for at least 1 hour or up to 8 hours, turning the venison occasionally.

2. To make the relish, put all the ingredients in a large saucepan with 2 tablespoons red wine marinade from the venison. Simmer for about 15 minutes or until the cranberries are soft. Adjust the sweetness, if necessary.

3. Lift the venison from the remaining marinade and dry on absorbent kitchen paper. Heat the butter and oil in a frying pan, add the venison and brown quickly. Lower the heat and cook for a further 4 minutes on each side. Season and serve with the relish.

— CHAPTER FOUR —

Meat

MEAT consumption is falling, but meat is still the centrepiece of many a dinner party. Buy the best you can find, which usually means finding a good butcher who you can rely on and who you can ask for advice. He will know the animals he buys and hang them for the appropriate times at the correct temperatures. Tender cuts are needed for quick cooking.

A bright red colour is not an indication of quality in beef, but of the length of time the carcass has been hung and how long the piece has been cut. Well-hung beef is a deeper red and dulls quite quickly after cutting.

Lamb is a tender meat. The flavour varies with the breed, where it was raised – mountain and hill lamb has a richer flavour than lowland lamb – and the age. The younger the lamb, the paler the colour and the milder the flavour.

Pork is also a tender meat and it is now much leaner than it used to be (some cuts can be leaner than chicken); it often has so little fat that it easily becomes dry when cooked unless care is taken. To avoid dryness, marinate pork in a marinade that contains oil. Very lean pork also usually lacks flavour so either add plenty of flavourings to the marinade or include them during the cooking.

If you don't have a meat thermometer to tell the degree to which meat is cooked, the following is a guide: When it is very rare to blue, it will offer no resistance when pressed; rare meat will be spongy when pressed; medium rare meat resists pressure; and well-done meat is firm. But remember that meat will continue to cook after it has been removed from the heat so it is particularly important to take care that you do not overcook it. This is especially the case when cooking joints that have to be rested before they are carved (to allow the juices to 'settle' and to prevent excessive juice being lost when the meat is cut).

SAUTÉED WHOLE FILLET OF BEEF WITH CHINESE MARINADE

•

— SERVES 6 —

F ILLET of beef is not usually associated with Chinese-style dishes, but this marinade gives it a good, rich flavour, as well as keeping it succulent. Whole pieces of meat cook better than individual pieces. This recipe makes use of the thin tail end of a piece of fillet of beef, which is too thin to roast but can be cooked quickly on the hob. Although fillet of beef is usually one of the most expensive cuts of meat, if not *the* most expensive, some butchers sell the tail end more cheaply.

2 pieces of tail end of beef fillet, each
   weighing 450–600g (1–1¼lb)
4 garlic cloves, crushed
5cm (2 inch) piece of fresh root ginger,
   grated
6 spring onions, thinly sliced
2 tablespoons dark soy sauce
4 tablespoons sherry vinegar

1 tablespoon sesame oil
3 tablespoons clear honey
1 teaspoon Chinese five-spice powder
1 teaspoon ground coriander
a few drops of Tabasco sauce
toasted sesame seeds and coriander leaves
   for garnish

1. Put the beef in a shallow dish that it just fits. Mix together the remaining ingredients, except the sesame seeds and coriander leaves, and pour over the beef. Turn the fillets to coat in the marinade, cover and leave overnight in the refrigerator.

2. Return the meat to room temperature 1 hour before cooking. Remove it from the marinade and pat it dry. Reserve the marinade.

3. Heat a lightly oiled, heavy-based frying pan, add the beef and fry for 5 minutes, pressing the meat down firmly on to the pan with a fish slice. Turn the meat over and cook for a further 3–4 minutes. Transfer the meat to a warm plate and keep warm.

4. Strain the marinade into the pan and boil until syrupy. Slice the meat and pour over the sauce. Sprinkle with sesame seeds and scatter over some coriander leaves before serving.

STEAKS WITH BÉARNAISE SAUCE

·

THIS classic dish is not often served at home (nor in all that many restaurants nowadays) but it is always popular, and with the help of a blender or food processor, Béarnaise sauce can be made extremely easily with little danger of curdling. It really is worth using chervil if you can, but if it proves too difficult to come by, substitute parsley.

6 rump steaks, each weighing about 175g (6oz)

coarsely ground black pepper

BÉARNAISE SAUCE
175g (6oz) unsalted butter, diced
1 shallot, finely chopped
150ml (5fl oz) dry white wine

2 tablespoons tarragon vinegar
4–6 black peppercorns, crushed
3 egg yolks
2 tablespoons chopped tarragon
2 tablespoons chopped chervil
salt

1. Preheat the grill. Season the steaks on both sides with coarsely ground black pepper, then grill for $2\frac{1}{4}$ minutes on each side for meat that is pink in the centre.

2. Meanwhile, to make the Béarnaise, gently melt the butter, then remove from the heat and keep warm. While the butter is melting, bring the shallot, wine, vinegar and peppercorns to the boil in a saucepan, then cook until the liquid has reduced to about 1 tablespoon. Remove from the heat and add 2 tablespoons water. Strain into a blender or food processor, add the egg yolks and mix briefly. With the motor running, pour in the butter in a slow steady stream until the sauce is emulsified and thick. Season with salt and add the herbs.

3. Serve the steaks with the warm sauce.

STEAKS WITH HORSERADISH RELISH

·

—— SERVES 6 ——

THIS recipe gives a new look to the old theme of beef and horseradish. The cooking time is for meat that is medium rare. Add a further 3–5 minutes if you prefer meat well done.

·

6 sirloin steaks, each weighing 175–200g (6–7oz)
3 tablespoons soy sauce
3 tablespoons sunflower oil
freshly ground black pepper

HORSERADISH RELISH
3 tablespoons creamed horseradish

1½ tablespoons soy sauce
1¼ tablespoons wholegrain mustard
6 tablespoons mayonnaise
2 spring onions, white parts only, finely sliced
1 small garlic clove, finely crushed
1¼ tablespoons chopped parsley
salt and freshly ground black pepper

·

1. Marinate the steaks in the soy sauce, sunflower oil and black pepper for 30–60 minutes, turning the steaks occasionally.

2. Meanwhile, stir together all the relish ingredients. Season and leave at room temperature until required.

3. Heat a ridged cast-iron frying pan, or a heavy-based frying pan. Remove the steaks from the marinade and cook briskly on both sides until browned. Reduce the heat to moderate and cook the steaks for a further 3–5 minutes, depending on size.

4. Leave the steaks to rest in a warm place for about 5 minutes before serving with the relish.

BEEF AND BROCCOLI STIR-FRY

·

—— SERVES 6 ——

LIKE all stir-fries, this one is quick to cook at the last minute, but unlike the majority of stir-fries, the recipe does not call for a lot of time-consuming and fiddly cutting before cooking can commence. Only the meat has to be cut into strips, and that is done at least 1 hour in advance so it has time to marinate.

juice and pared rind of 1 large orange	250g (9oz) egg noodles
6 tablespoons sherry	3 tablespoons groundnut oil
3 tablespoons dark soy sauce	1 bunch of spring onions, chopped
1½ teaspoons cornflour	3 garlic cloves, finely crushed
1½ teaspoons sugar	5 slices of fresh root ginger
6 teaspoons sesame oil	1–2 red chillies, deseeded and thinly sliced
350g (12oz) rump steak, cut into thin	250g (9oz) broccoli florets
finger-length strips	freshly ground black pepper

1. Mix together the orange rind, sherry, soy sauce, cornflour, sugar and 2 teaspoons sesame oil. Add the beef and marinate for at least 1 hour or overnight.

2. Cook the noodles in boiling salted water according to the directions on the packet. Drain well.

3. Lift the meat from the marinade with a slotted spoon, reserving the marinade. Heat the groundnut oil in a large frying pan (preferably non-stick) or wok, add the beef and stir-fry until browned and cooked to your liking. Remove and keep warm.

4. Add the spring onions, garlic, ginger and chillies to the pan, fry for 1 minute, then add the broccoli and stir-fry for 2–3 minutes.

5. Pour the reserved marinade and the orange juice into the pan, add the noodles and beef, and bubble for 2–3 minutes. Season with black pepper and serve sprinkled with the remaining sesame oil.

BRITISH VEAL KEBAB ROLLS

·

—— SERVES 6 ——

BRITISH veal calves are not reared in inhumane crates, so their flesh is more tasty and has colour. The rolls can be served with Red Pepper and Tomato Sauce (see page 96) or Tomato and Red Pepper Salsa (see page 100).

6 British veal escalopes, total weight about
   450g (1lb)
6 slices of smoked ham
soft cheese with garlic and herbs for
   spreading
5 tablespoons virgin olive oil

2 tablespoons lemon juice
1 tablespoon chopped rosemary
about 50g (2oz) coarsely grated Parmesan
   cheese, or crumbled feta cheese
freshly ground black pepper

1. Beat out the veal escalopes in turn between two sheets of greaseproof paper or clingfilm. Lay a slice of ham on top of each escalope, and spread with soft cheese. Roll up and cut each roll into four slices. Put into a non-metallic dish. Pour over the oil and lemon juice, add the rosemary and black pepper, cover and leave for 2 hours, or overnight, turning the rolls occasionally.

2. Preheat the grill. Thread the rolls on to six skewers and grill for about 12 minutes, turning occasionally and brushing with the marinade. Sprinkle over the cheese and grill for a further minute.

LAMB CUTLETS WITH PROVENÇAL VEGETABLES

·

—— SERVES 6 ——

QUITE a large grill area is needed to cook all the lamb cutlets in one go, and you will probably have to move them around so that they are all cooked at the same time. If you do not have a large grill, and would prefer not to cook the lamb in batches, use 12 lamb noisettes and cook them for 5 minutes on each side.

18 lamb cutlets
150ml (5fl oz) olive oil
juice of 1 lemon
2 thyme sprigs
salt and freshly ground black pepper
basil leaves for garnish

PROVENÇAL VEGETABLES
4 tablespoons olive oil

1 largish onion, chopped
3 garlic cloves, peeled but left whole
1 small red pepper
1 small yellow pepper
2 small courgettes
leaves from a large bunch of basil, chopped
40g (1½oz) Parmesan cheese, freshly grated
salt and freshly ground black pepper

1. Put the lamb in a shallow dish and pour over the oil and lemon juice. Add the thyme sprigs. Turn the lamb over, cover the dish and leave for 30–60 minutes.

2. Meanwhile, prepare the vegetables. Heat 2 tablespoons of the oil in a large frying pan, add the onion and cook gently until softened but not coloured, adding the garlic towards the end of cooking.

3. While the onion is cooking, dice the peppers and dice the courgettes. Add to the softened onion and cook for about 15 minutes or until softened; do not allow them to colour.

4. Preheat the grill. Grill the lamb for about 3 minutes on each side, until pink in the centre. Season.

5. Tip the vegetable mixture into a blender or food processor and mix to a very coarse purée. Return to the pan, add the basil, remaining oil, the cheese and seasoning, and warm through.

6. Serve the vegetables with the lamb, and garnish with basil leaves.

FILLET OF LAMB WITH PIQUANT MAYONNAISE

•

—— SERVES 4 ——

THE sauce can be made in advance and kept in a screw-topped jar in the refrigerator for a few days; in fact, the flavour improves if it is made a little while ahead so I make it one of the first things I do when preparing the meal. Alternatively, it can easily be made in the time it takes for the lamb to cook.

2 fillets of lamb, each weighing about 350g (12oz)
1 plump garlic clove, halved
olive oil for brushing
freshly ground black pepper

PIQUANT MAYONNAISE
2 egg yolks
2 garlic cloves

1 teaspoon Dijon mustard
4 teaspoons lime juice
300ml ($\frac{1}{2}$ pint) olive oil
$2\frac{1}{2}$ tablespoons capers, chopped
4 small gherkins, finely chopped
$2\frac{1}{2}$ tablespoons chopped tarragon
$2\frac{1}{2}$ tablespoons chopped parsley
freshly ground black pepper

1. Preheat the oven to 230°C/450°F/gas 8. Rub the lamb with the cut side of the garlic, season with black pepper and brush with olive oil. Heat a large, dry frying pan, add the lamb and sear all over. Transfer to a roasting tin and roast in the oven for 8–10 minutes or until the lamb is cooked but still pink in the centre.

2. Meanwhile, make the piquant mayonnaise. Put the egg yolks, garlic, mustard and half of the lime juice in a small blender and mix together briefly. With the motor running, very slowly pour in the oil until half has been added, then pour in the remainder slightly more quickly. Add the remaining lime juice, then transfer to a bowl. Stir in the remaining ingredients.

3. Allow the lamb to rest in a warm place for 5 minutes before slicing on the diagonal. Serve with the piquant mayonnaise.

NOISETTES OF LAMB WITH TWO TOMATO AND BASIL SAUCE

·

—— SERVES 4 ——

SUN-DRIED tomatoes and the oil from the jar of sun-dried tomatoes produce a sauce that has depth of flavour. It can be made in advance, if liked, and the lamb can be coated in the crumbs ahead of the cooking time so it is ready to put in the oven when called for.

·

25g (1oz) unsalted butter, melted
75g (3oz) fresh breadcrumbs
1 tablespoon finely chopped rosemary
8 lamb noisettes
1 egg, beaten
salt and freshly ground black pepper

SAUCE
4 well-flavoured tomatoes

1½ tablespoons oil from the jar of sun-dried tomatoes, or olive oil
1 garlic clove, crushed
1 red onion, finely chopped
6 sun-dried tomatoes in oil, drained
5 tablespoons medium-bodied dry white wine
1 tablespoon chopped basil
salt and freshly ground black pepper

·

1. Preheat the oven to 220°C/425°F/gas 7. Mix together the butter, breadcrumbs, rosemary and seasoning. Brush the noisettes lightly with beaten egg, then cover evenly with the breadcrumb mixture, pressing it on firmly. Place in a baking dish and bake in the oven for about 15 minutes or until cooked but still pink in the centre.

2. Meanwhile, to make the sauce, peel and chop the fresh tomatoes. Heat the oil in a saucepan, add the garlic and red onion, and fry gently for 2–3 minutes.

3. While the garlic is frying, chop the sun-dried tomatoes. Add both types of tomatoes and the wine to the fried garlic and red onion. Simmer for 15 minutes, stirring occasionally. Just before serving, add the basil and seasoning.

4. Serve the sauce with the noisettes.

LAMB WITH GREEN OLIVE TAPENADE TOPPING

•

— SERVES 6 —

CHOOSE thin, wide pieces of lamb for this dish so the topping can be spread out well, and for quicker cooking. I use firm bread as it has more flavour and gives the topping a better texture; if you use soft sliced bread there is no need to soak it as it contains enough moisture.

6 lamb steaks, each weighing 175–200g (6–7oz)

1 lemon, cut into 6 slices

TAPENADE
1½ slices of day-old bread
2 garlic cloves
40g (1½oz) flaked almonds

125g (4½oz) pitted green olives
3 tablespoons capers
3 anchovy fillets
6 tablespoons olive oil
juice of 1 lemon
freshly ground black pepper

1. Preheat the oven to 190°C/375°F/gas 5. If you are using dry, quite firm bread for the tapenade, leave it to soak in enough water to moisten it. Meanwhile, oil a shallow baking dish large enough to hold the lamb in a single layer (or use two dishes), and put the lamb in it.

2. Squeeze the bread dry. With the motor running, drop the garlic into a blender and chop coarsely. Add the almonds, olives, capers, anchovy fillets and bread, and mix until coarsely chopped. Slowly pour in the oil. Add lemon juice and plenty of black pepper to taste (salt should not be necessary).

3. Spoon the olive mixture on to the lamb steaks and top each one with a slice of lemon. Bake for 7–8 minutes.

LAMB WITH MIDDLE-EASTERN AUBERGINE PURÉE

·

—— SERVES 4 ——

THE affinity of lamb and aubergines was discovered long ago in Middle-Eastern countries. The method I give here is the quickest one for making this recipe. As the oven has to be on, you could bake the aubergines instead of grilling them, putting them in the oven either when it is hot or while it is heating up, but they will take longer. Another way to make the dish is to brown the lamb and put it into the oven to cook before making the purée.

2 fillets of lamb, each weighing about
   350g (12oz)
2 tablespoons extra-virgin olive oil
freshly ground black pepper

AUBERGINE PURÉE
2 aubergines
2–3 tablespoons olive oil, plus extra for
   brushing

2–3 garlic cloves, unpeeled (optional)
2 teaspoons lightly toasted cumin seeds,
   crushed
17–20 mint leaves
about 2 tablespoons lemon juice
salt and freshly ground black pepper
coriander sprigs for garnish (optional)

1. Brush the lamb with the oil and season with black pepper. Leave for 30 minutes.

2. Preheat the oven to 230°C/450°F/gas 8, and preheat the grill. Slice the aubergines lengthways into quarters, score the flesh a few times, sprinkle with black pepper and brush with oil. Grill the aubergines and garlic, if using, turning as necessary, until soft and the aubergine is lightly browned, taking care not to let the aubergine get too soft. Peel the garlic, then purée in a blender with the aubergine (including the skin), cumin, 2–3 tablespoons olive oil, mint, lemon juice and seasoning. I like to leave a little texture in the purée. Reheat gently.

3. Meanwhile, heat a large, heavy-based frying pan. When it is very hot, add the lamb and brown quickly on both sides. Transfer to a roasting tin and roast for 8–10 minutes or until cooked but still pink inside.

4. Leave the lamb to stand in a warm place for 5 minutes, then slice diagonally and serve with the purée, which can be garnished with coriander sprigs.

ROAST LAMB WITH PIQUANT HERB COATING

•

— SERVES 6 —

R ACK of lamb is one roast on the bone that can be cooked in under 30 minutes if you like pink (and that doesn't mean bloody) lamb. If you prefer lamb that is more well done, add another 5–7 minutes.

3 tablespoons chopped mixed herbs, such as thyme, parsley, chives, mint and sage
1 tablespoon black olive paste
1 tablespoon Dijon mustard
4 tablespoons fresh white breadcrumbs
4 tablespoons olive oil

3 prepared racks of lamb, each with 6 bones
300ml (½ pint) medium-bodied dry white wine
salt and freshly ground black pepper

1. Preheat the oven to 220°C/425°F/gas 7.

2. Mix together the herbs, black olive paste, mustard, breadcrumbs, 2 tablespoons olive oil and seasoning. Spread over the fat of the lamb and stand, crumb-side up, in a roasting tin.

3. Pour the remaining oil over the coating and roast for about 25 minutes or until the coating is crisp and the lamb is pink.

4. Transfer the lamb to a warm plate and keep warm.

5. Stir the wine and a little water into the roasting tin to dislodge the cooking juices, then place on the hob and boil until reduced to a thin gravy. Check the seasoning, and serve with the lamb.

ROAST LAMB WITH TOMATO AND THYME COATING

•

—— SERVES 6 ——

A SIMPLE gravy can be made to serve with the lamb as with Roast Lamb with Piquant Herb Coating on page 74. To make this virtually a one-pot dish, you could add the vegetables as in the Italian Roast Chicken and Vegetables on page 48.

115g (4oz) sun-dried tomatoes in oil,
   drained
2 tablespoons oil from the jar of sun-dried
   tomatoes
2 garlic cloves

1 teaspoon chopped thyme
3 prepared racks of lamb, each with 6
   bones
salt and freshly ground black pepper

1. Preheat the oven to 220°C/425°F/gas 7. Put the sun-dried tomatoes, sun-dried tomato oil, garlic, thyme and seasoning in a blender and mix to a paste.

2. Score the fat of the lamb. Press the tomato mixture firmly into the lamb to coat it. Put in a roasting tin and roast for 25 minutes. If the coating becomes too brown, cover the lamb with foil.

3. Allow the lamb to stand in a warm place for 5–10 minutes before serving.

BUTTERFLY LEG OR SHOULDER OF LAMB

•

THE lamb takes 50–55 minutes to cook for medium rare, but it can be left to cook in the oven, and only occasionally needs basting.

900g (2lb) boned shoulder or leg of lamb
3 garlic cloves, cut into slivers

MARINADE
115ml (4fl oz) dry sherry

115ml (4fl oz) light soy sauce
1 tablespoon clear honey
seeds from 2 star anise, lightly crushed
1½ tablespoons chopped coriander

1. Open out the lamb. Cut some slits in the meat, insert the slivers of garlic, and put in a non-metallic dish. Mix all the marinade ingredients together and pour over the lamb. Turn the lamb over, cover and leave for 8 hours, turning occasionally.

2. Preheat the oven to 230°C/450°F/gas 8. Transfer the lamb to a roasting tin, reserving the marinade. Roast in the oven for 25 minutes, then lower the oven temperature to 180°C/350°F/gas 4 and roast for a further 20–25 minutes. Baste frequently throughout the cooking.

PORK COLLOPS WITH ARTICHOKES AND MUSHROOMS

•

—— SERVES 4 ——

TAGLIATELLE is a good accompaniment.

450g (1lb) jar of artichokes preserved in
   oil
juice of 1 lemon
2 pork fillets, each weighing about 350g
   (12oz)
225g (8oz) oyster mushrooms

5 tablespoons dry white vermouth
150ml (5fl oz) crème fraîche
2 teaspoons chopped sage
salt and freshly ground black pepper

1. Drain the artichokes, reserving the oil. Mix 2 tablespoons of the oil with half of the lemon juice. Cut each pork fillet into six collops and brush with the lemon and oil. Leave at room temperature for about 1 hour, turning occasionally.

2. Meanwhile, thinly slice the artichokes and mushrooms.

3. Preheat the grill. Heat $1\frac{1}{2}$ tablespoons of the remaining reserved artichoke oil in a saucepan, add the artichokes and mushrooms, and cook over a low heat, stirring occasionally, until the mushrooms are almost tender. Add the vermouth and boil hard until reduced by half. Stir in the crème fraîche and boil, stirring frequently, until thickened.

4. Add the sage, seasoning, and remaining lemon juice if necessary.

5. Grill the pork for about 5 minutes on each side until cooked through.

6. Slice each collop into three and serve some of the sauce with each portion of pork.

PORK COLLOPS WITH CRANBERRY AND APPLE RELISH

·

—— SERVES 6 ——

N ow that pork is as lean as other meats, a sharp, fruity accompaniment is no longer needed to counteract its richness, but in this recipe the lightly spiced cranberry and apple relish really lifts the mild flavour of lean pork fillets. This is a very quick and easy dish to prepare.

·

3 pork fillets, each weighing about 350g
  (12oz)
olive oil for brushing
350g (12oz) apple purée

225g (8oz) fresh or frozen cranberries
$\frac{1}{2}$ teaspoon mixed spice
salt and freshly ground black pepper

·

1. Cut each pork fillet into six collops. Brush with olive oil, sprinkle with black pepper, and set aside. Preheat the grill.

2. Pour the apple purée into a saucepan. Stir in the cranberries and mixed spice, and simmer for 15 minutes, stirring occasionally. Season.

3. Grill the pork collops for 6–8 minutes on each side or until cooked through. Season with salt.

4. Serve the collops with the relish.

OPPOSITE: Italian Roast Chicken and Vegetables (page 48) and Golden Potatoes (page 86)

PORK NOISETTES WITH APPLE AND SAGE RELISH

·

—— SERVES 6 ——

LOOK for pork noisettes in the supermarket, or ask a butcher to prepare them.

·

6 pork noisettes, each weighing 175–
200g (6–7oz)
olive oil for brushing
2 teaspoons finely chopped sage
freshly ground black pepper

APPLE AND SAGE RELISH
225 g (1oz) unsalted butter

1 large onion, finely chopped
2 Bramley apples
1 tablespoon finely chopped sage
grated zest of $\frac{1}{4}$ lemon
1 tablespoon white wine vinegar
about 1 teaspoon sugar
salt and freshly ground black pepper

1. Lightly brush the noisettes with oil and sprinkle with sage and black pepper.

2. To make the relish, heat the butter in a large saucepan, add the onion, and fry until softened but not coloured.

3. Meanwhile, peel and core the apples and cut into chunks. Stir into the softened onions with the sage, lemon zest and vinegar, and add sugar and seasoning to taste. Cover tightly and cook gently, shaking the pan occasionally to prevent sticking, until the apples are tender.

4. While the apples are cooking, preheat the grill. Grill the pork noisettes for 6–7 minutes on each side until the juices run clear when the noisettes are pierced with a sharp fine knife.

5. Serve the noisettes with the relish.

OPPOSITE: Baked Duck Breasts with Tropical Salsa (page 58)

PORK ROULADES WITH FETA AND HERB FILLING

•

—— SERVES 6 ——

To save time on the evening of the dinner party, the roulades can be prepared in advance and kept covered in the refrigerator. Remove them to room temperature about 1 hour before cooking. Mashed potatoes, or puréed celeriac or cauliflower are good accompaniments.

2 pork fillets, each weighing about 350g (12oz)
50g (2oz) unsalted butter, diced
1 onion, quite finely chopped
1 garlic clove
3 tablespoons chopped basil
6 tablespoons chopped parsley

175g (6oz) feta cheese
200ml (7fl oz) medium-bodied dry white wine
200ml (7fl oz) chicken stock
200ml (7fl oz) crème fraîche
salt and freshly ground black pepper

1. Slice across each pork fillet to make six pieces. Place each of the 12 pieces in turn between two sheets of clingfilm and bat out to about 3mm ($\frac{1}{8}$ inch) thick.

2. Heat the butter in a deep frying pan, add the onion and fry until softened but not coloured.

3. Meanwhile, crush the garlic and add to the onion towards the end of cooking.

4. Mix 1–2 tablespoons of the basil, half the parsley, and black pepper into the cheese until evenly combined. Spread over each piece of pork, then roll up and secure with wooden cocktail sticks.

5. Add the rolls to the pan and brown all over. Pour in the wine, stock and crème fraîche, and add the remaining herbs. Bring to the boil, then cover and simmer for 10–15 minutes or until the pork is tender. Season to taste.

6. Serve the roulades sliced or whole.

PORK WITH RHUBARB RELISH

·

—— SERVES 6 ——

The character of the relish can be changed depending on whether you use white, demerara or light soft brown sugar; the lighter the sugar, the lighter, fresher tasting the relish. For another change of character, replace the rhubarb with the same amount of chopped, peeled and cored cooking apples.

·

3 pork fillets, each weighing about 350g (12oz)

juice of 2 lemons

3 tablespoons olive oil, plus extra for frying

salt and freshly ground black pepper

RHUBARB RELISH

125g (4½oz) sugar

125ml (4½fl oz) cider vinegar

500g (18oz) rhubarb stalks, chopped

1 red onion, quite finely chopped

1 small garlic clove, finely crushed

125g (4½oz) raisins

2cm (¾ inch) piece of fresh root ginger, grated

generous ½ teaspoon ground cinnamon

¼ teaspoon ground cloves

salt and freshly ground black pepper

1. Put the pork in a shallow non-metallic dish. Pour over the lemon juice and 3 tablespoons oil, season with black pepper and turn the meat over. Cover and marinate for at least 1 hour or up to 4 hours, basting occasionally.

2. Heat some oil for frying in a large frying pan. Lift the pork from the marinade and brown quickly in the oil. Transfer to a shallow baking dish, pour over the marinade and bake in the oven for 20 minutes, basting occasionally.

3. Towards the end of the cooking time, make the relish. Gently heat the sugar in the vinegar until dissolved. Add the remaining ingredients and bring to the boil. Simmer for 5 minutes, stirring gently occasionally, until the rhubarb is just tender but not falling apart. Keep warm but take care not to let the rhubarb overcook.

4. Leave the pork in a warm place for 5 minutes. Season the pork and cut into medallions. Serve with the relish.

CHAPTER FIVE

Accompaniments & Extras

T HE RECIPES in this chapter are those accompaniments that I find
particularly versatile, including sauces and pastes as well as vegetables. Also included are some recipes that will add something
extra to the meal, such as Cornmeal Muffins and Crunchy Cheese Bites.
These are useful to give to guests if I know that the meal isn't going to be
ready soon after they arrive, or if I am simply running behind time in the
kitchen. If I think ahead, and have time, I make a batch in advance and
keep them in the freezer ready to pop in the oven before guests arrive.

Accompaniments should complement the style of the main dish; if it has
a rich sauce or is highly spiced, avoid serving sauced or spicy vegetables,
but if the main dish is plain, or fairly plain, select imaginative accompaniments. Avoid serving all sauced or highly seasoned dishes, or dishes with
flavours that 'clash', such as a Chinese-style dish, a curry and pasta tossed
with Mediterranean ingredients. Even though they may all be so delicious
that you want to show them off to your guests, together they present too
much of a jumble of flavours for any of them to be enjoyable.

Choosing a dish that has its own vegetables, such as Italian Roast Chicken
and Vegetables (see page 49) means all the cooking can be done together
in the oven, so you will have less to think about, and you will save space
on the hob and cut down on washing-up. If the rest of the meal involves
quite a lot of work or pots and pans, opt for a salad to serve with the main
course. The same applies if you are very short of time. The dressing for the
salad can be made in advance but do not dress the salad leaves until just
before serving.

A tiered steamer allows you to use just one ring or burner to cook two
or more vegetables, and saves the palaver of straining the vegetables. They
can also sit in the steamer with the heat turned off and keep warm for a
while after they are cooked, whereas boiled vegetables have to be strained
straight away. I use an electric steamer because the shape and size of the

basket is not restricted by having to be put on a saucepan; it is an oval with blunt ends and large enough to spread out enough vegetables to serve six in a single, or at least shallow layer.

Vegetables simply steamed or boiled can be dressed up with spices (try, for example, grated nutmeg with sprouts), tossed with a French dressing or mayonnaise, perhaps blended with cream or soft cheese, soft cheese with herbs, Red Pepper Pesto, Tomato and Red Pepper Salsa and, of course, butter; this could be flavoured with pesto, Red Pepper Pesto or Tapenade with Sun-dried Tomatoes.

'ROAST' POTATOES WITH GARLIC AND ROSEMARY

·

—— SERVES 4–6 ——

'ROAST' is in inverted commas because the potatoes are cooked on the hob rather than in the oven. As they cook more quickly than conventional roast potatoes they are useful for the cook in a hurry who wants to serve a roast meal, partnering the potatoes with, for example, either of the rack of lamb recipes on pages 74–75.

900g (2lb) potatoes, quartered	2 rosemary sprigs
100ml (3½fl oz) olive oil	20g (¾oz) unsalted butter
1 garlic clove, halved lengthways	salt and freshly ground black pepper

1. Wash and dry the prepared potatoes. Heat the oil in a non-stick pan that is large enough to hold the potatoes in a single layer. Add the potatoes and garlic, cover and cook gently, shaking the pan occasionally, for about 30 minutes or until the potatoes are almost tender.

2. Add the rosemary and butter, and cook until the potatoes are tender and golden brown, increasing the heat if necessary. Season to taste before serving.

GOLDEN POTATOES

·

—— SERVES 6 ——

THESE fragrantly glowing potatoes will make any meal special, but they are particularly good with fish, shellfish, chicken and guinea fowl dishes that do not have a conflicting sauce.

·

900g (2lb) potatoes, unpeeled
1 teaspoon saffron strands, crushed

about 40g (1½oz) unsalted butter
salt and freshly ground black pepper

·

1. Cut the potatoes into even 1–2cm (½–¾ inch) chunks. Put into a saucepan with the saffron, just cover with water and bring to the boil. Cover and simmer for about 10 minutes or until almost tender.

2. Uncover the pan and boil the potatoes for 5–10 minutes or until they are just tender and most of the liquid has evaporated. Add the butter and continue to boil until the potatoes are coated with a golden yellow glaze. Season and serve.

WHITE BEANS WITH SALSA VERDE

·

—— SERVES 6 ——

THE effectiveness of this dish lies in the contrast between the hot, white, mild-flavoured beans and the cold, green, robustly flavoured sauce. The parsley and bay leaf can be scooped out of the beans before serving, if liked. Serve with pork, lamb, chicken and game dishes.

2 garlic cloves, crushed
1 onion, quite finely chopped
several parsley sprigs
1 bay leaf, torn
two 400g (14oz) cans of cannellini or
   haricot beans, drained and rinsed

SALSA VERDE
2 garlic cloves

4 anchovy fillets
1 tablespoon capers
leaves from a bunch of parsley
leaves from a small bunch of basil
10 mint leaves
1 tablespoon Dijon mustard
115ml (4fl oz) virgin olive oil
freshly ground black pepper

1. Put the crushed garlic, the onion, parsley, bay leaf and beans in a saucepan and add just enough water to cover. Bring to the boil, then cover the pan and simmer for about 5 minutes to warm through.

2. Meanwhile, make the salsa verde. Put all the ingredients except the pepper, using about a quarter of the oil, in a blender, and process to a coarse purée. With the motor running, slowly pour in the remaining oil. Do not overmix as the sauce should be quite coarse. Season with pepper.

3. Drain the beans and tip into a warm serving dish. Spoon a good dollop of the salsa verde on top and serve. Serve the remaining salsa verde separately.

BUTTER BEAN PURÉE

•

— SERVES 6 —

THIS purée goes well with lamb, pork or duck. If liked, it can be enriched with a good knob of unsalted butter, stirred in when the purée is being reheated.

150ml (5fl oz) vegetable stock or water
3 garlic cloves, crushed
two 400g (14oz) cans of butter beans,
   drained and rinsed

1 lemon
2 tablespoons chopped parsley
salt and freshly ground black pepper

1. Put the stock or water and the garlic into a saucepan and bring to the boil. Add the beans, then simmer until the beans are disintegrating.

2. Meanwhile, grate the zest from the lemon and squeeze the juice.

3. Purée the contents of the saucepan in a blender, or food processor and return to the pan. Add the lemon zest and juice, the parsley and seasoning. Heat through. If necessary, adjust the consistency of the purée with more stock or water.

BROCCOLI WITH OLIVE OIL HOLLANDAISE SAUCE

·

—— SERVES 4 ——

USING olive oil instead of butter makes a more healthy, though not less fattening, Hollandaise sauce. As with conventional Hollandaise, it can quickly and easily be made in a blender, and goes superbly with broccoli.

450g (1lb) broccoli florets

OLIVE OIL HOLLANDAISE SAUCE
150ml (5fl oz) mild olive oil
1 large egg yolk

1 teaspoon Dijon mustard
a few drops of lemon juice
salt and freshly ground white or black pepper

1. To make the sauce, warm the oil but do not let it get too hot. Put the egg yolk, mustard, lemon juice and a pinch of salt in a small blender. With the motor running, very slowly pour the oil into the blender until about half of the oil has been added, then it can be poured in slightly more quickly. If the sauce becomes too thick, add a little hot water. Season, adding more mustard and lemon juice, if necessary. Cover and keep warm.

2. Bring a kettle of water to the boil. Put the broccoli in a wide saucepan, add enough water to cover by 1cm ($\frac{1}{2}$ inch) and boil hard for 1–2 minutes. Drain well, and tip into a warm serving dish. Serve with the sauce.

BAKED BABY AUBERGINES

·

INSTEAD of the *gremolata* topping, the aubergines can be spread with pesto, red pesto, black olive paste, or topped with a mixture of freshly grated Parmesan cheese, breadcrumbs, and some parsley or chives, if liked. Dishes the aubergines can be served with include any of the lamb dishes (except perhaps Lamb Cutlets with Provençal Vegetables and Lamb with Middle-Eastern Aubergine Purée, see pages 69 and 73), the veal rolls on page 68, Crisp Monkfish Packages (see page 38) and Red Snapper with Provençal Salsa (see page 39).

9 baby aubergines	3 tablespoons chopped coriander or
olive oil for brushing	parsley
1 small garlic clove	salt and freshly ground black pepper
1 lemon	

1. Preheat the oven to 200°C/400°F/gas 6. Cut the aubergines in half lengthways and score the flesh. Brush with olive oil and bake in the oven for about 20 minutes or until almost tender.

2. Meanwhile, finely chop the garlic. Finely grate the zest from the lemon and squeeze out the juice. Mix the garlic, lemon zest and juice, coriander or parsley and seasoning.

3. Sprinkle the garlic mixture over the aubergines and return to the oven for about 10 minutes or until the aubergines are tender.

CUCUMBER AND MINT SALAD

·

—— SERVES 6 ——

THE herb can be changed to coriander or dill according to the dish the salad is to accompany. Although I often serve it as an accompaniment with, for example, Baby Salmon instead of Fennel Mayonnaise (see page 35), I also serve it as a light refreshing first course in summer. It can also be puréed to make a soup.

·

¾ large cucumber
1 garlic clove, crushed
225ml (8fl oz) Greek yogurt, chilled

2–3 tablespoons chopped mint, coriander, dill or whatever herb is appropriate
salt and freshly ground black pepper

·

Cut the cucumber in half lengthways and scoop out the seeds. Grate the cucumber into a bowl and stir in the remaining ingredients.

ARTICHOKE AND SUN-DRIED TOMATO RAGOUT

·

—— SERVES 6 ——

THIS makes a tasty and attractive accompaniment to simple roast or grilled pork, lamb or chicken. It can also be served as a first course or light main course, perhaps changing the *pancetta* or Parma ham to goats' or feta cheese. Whether the dish is served as an accompaniment or first course, the herb can be changed if another is more appropriate or preferred.

·

1½ teaspoons oil from the artichokes (see right)
75g (3oz) *pancetta* or Parma ham, quite finely chopped
1 small onion
1 garlic clove

585g (21oz) artichokes in oil
75g (3oz) sun-dried tomatoes in oil
2 tablespoons chopped parsley
salt and freshly ground black pepper

·

1. Heat the oil in a frying pan, add the *pancetta* or Parma ham, and fry until brown.

2. Meanwhile, chop the onion quite finely and crush the garlic. Add to the browned *pancetta* or ham and fry until softened but not coloured.

3. Drain and halve the artichokes. Drain and slice the sun-dried tomatoes.

4. Stir the artichokes, sun-dried tomatoes and parsley into the pan, season and cover the pan. Heat through, shaking the pan occasionally.

GRILLED CHICORY

•

CHICORY can too easily be spoilt by sogginess, but this recipe overcomes this, providing you drain and dry the chicory well in stage 3. A mixture of freshly grated Parmesan cheese, or finely crumbled goats' or feta cheese, and breadcrumbs can be sprinkled over the chicory for a savoury topping.

8 small heads of chicory, total weight about 600g (1¼lb)	2 tablespoons olive oil salt and freshly ground black pepper

1. Bring a large saucepan of water to the boil. Halve the chicory heads lengthways, add to the boiling water and boil for 1 minute.

2. Preheat the grill.

3. Drain the chicory well and pat dry with absorbent kitchen paper. Place cut-side down on a large oiled baking sheet or shallow baking dish, season and brush with oil. Grill for 3–4 minutes or until golden. Turn over and grill the second side until golden, or lightly charred if you prefer.

SESAME AND CORIANDER NOODLES

·

ALTHOUGH these noodles have an oriental flavour, I do not only serve them with Eastern-style recipes as I find they go well with all manner of dishes, and make a nice change. They can be turned into a first course or light lunch or supper dish by tossing with prawns, finely crumbled feta or goats' cheese, chopped Parma ham, chopped fried or grilled red peppers or cooked asparagus.

450g (1lb) medium egg noodles
1 tablespoon sesame oil
4 tablespoons chopped coriander

salt and freshly ground black pepper
toasted sesame seeds for tossing
 (optional)

1. Cook the noodles in a large saucepan of boiling water with half of the sesame oil, according to the directions on the packet.

2. Drain well and toss with the coriander, seasoning, remaining sesame oil and sesame seeds, if using.

OPPOSITE: Roast Lamb with Piquant Herb Coating (page 74) and Artichoke and Sundried Tomato Ragout (page 92)

COUSCOUS

•

—— SERVES 6 ——

COUSCOUS has an affinity with most other ingredients and flavours, so offers a lot of scope for making into interesting and appropriate accompaniments. Any herb or spice, chopped dried fruits, nuts, grated cheese, members of the onion family, sun-dried tomatoes, capers, olives or cooked vegetables are just some of the ingredients that can be added. The couscous sold nowadays is much quicker to prepare than traditional couscous, as you can see from the method below.

about 450ml (16fl oz) boiling water
350g (12oz) couscous

unsalted butter or virgin olive oil
salt and freshly ground black pepper

1. Pour enough boiling water over the couscous to cover by about 2.5cm (1 inch), cover with foil, a plate or a lid and leave to soak for about 10 minutes or until the water is absorbed.

2. Stir a large knob of butter or 2–3 tablespoons oil into the couscous with seasoning to taste. Serve immediately.

OPPOSITE: Chocolate Amaretto Castles with Chocolate and Hazelnut Sauce (page 110)

RED PEPPER AND TOMATO SAUCE

·

—— SERVES 6 ——

I HAVE found that this sauce goes well with any meat, poultry or fish. It can be made in advance and kept covered in the refrigerator for a couple of days, then heated when required.

·

1½ tablespoons olive oil
1 red onion, finely chopped
1 garlic clove, crushed
2 red peppers, grilled if liked, chopped

4 well-flavoured tomatoes, chopped
2–3 teaspoons sun-dried tomato paste
1 tablespoon chopped basil or chives
salt and freshly ground black pepper

·

1. Heat the oil and fry the red onion and garlic until softened but not coloured. Add the red peppers, tomatoes and sun-dried tomato paste and 2 tablespoons water. Cook gently for about 10 minutes.

2. Allow the sauce to cool slightly, then purée in a blender. Return to the pan and heat through. Add the basil or chives, and seasoning.

TAPENADE WITH SUN-DRIED TOMATOES

•

MAKES ABOUT 200ml (7 fl oz)

THE main ingredient of the classic Provençal tapenade is capers (the name comes from the Provençal word for capers, *tapo*). Adjust the levels of the various ingredients to suit your taste. Use it to spread on crostini, to flavour Cornmeal Muffins (see page 104) or for Roast Monkfish with Parma Ham (see page 37). Keep it in a covered container with a little oil poured over the top, in a cool, dark place.

40g (1½oz) capers
225g (8oz) oil-cured black olives, pitted
25g (1oz) anchovy fillets
1 teaspoon Dijon mustard
4–6 tablespoons virgin olive oil
about 1½ teaspoons red wine vinegar

6 basil leaves, chopped
1½ tablespoons chopped parsley
1½ tablespoons finely chopped sun-dried
  tomatoes
freshly ground black pepper

1. Put the capers, olives, anchovy fillets, mustard, 4 tablespoons of the oil, and the vinegar into a small blender. Mix to a coarse purée.

2. Stir in the basil, parsley and sun-dried tomatoes, and add pepper to taste. Add a little more olive oil if liked.

PESTO

•

I KNOW fresh and bottled pesto is now readily available but the quality varies quite considerably. None can beat pesto made at home, providing first class raw ingredients are used. It takes only minutes to make using a blender or food processor and can be kept in the refrigerator for a few days if a thin layer of olive oil is spooned over the top of the sauce; stir in the oil before serving. The proportions of the ingredients can be varied according to taste.

2 cloves garlic, peeled
2 tablespoons pine nuts
about 15g ($\frac{1}{2}$oz) basil leaves
about 75ml (3fl oz) virgin olive oil, plus
   extra for brushing

3 tablespoons mixed freshly grated
   pecorino and Parmesan cheese, or all
   Parmesan cheese
freshly ground black pepper

Drop the garlic into a blender or food processor with the motor running, then add the pine nuts, basil leaves and oil. Mix until smooth and add the cheese. Mix very briefly. Season with black pepper.

RED PEPPER PESTO

•

THIS is a useful recipe because it can be made in advance and kept in a jar in the fridge for a few days. Float a spoonful of oil over the surface of the sauce, then stir in this oil just before using to add instant dash to pasta, rice or grilled or roast meats or fish. It can be spread on bruschetta or crostini or spooned on to creamed scrambled eggs.

2 garlic cloves
2 red peppers, grilled if liked, chopped
4 pieces of sun-dried tomato in oil, drained
2 tablespoons capers (optional)
75g (3oz) pine kernels

6–7 tablespoons virgin olive oil
75g (3oz) pecorino or Parmesan cheese, freshly grated
salt and freshly ground black pepper

Put the first five ingredients in a blender and mix together briefly. With the motor running, slowly pour in the oil. Add the cheese and season to taste.

TOMATO AND RED PEPPER SALSA

•

— SERVES 6 —

THIS recipe is a good starting point because there is plenty of scope for making changes or additions according to your taste or the dish the salsa is to accompany. For example, use lemon or lime juice instead of balsamic vinegar; add finely chopped chilli or chopped anchovies, black olives and/or capers. The salsa adds distinction to grilled meats, poultry and fish; can be spread on to toasted bread for crostini or bruschetta; served with eggs, or spooned on to a green salad or tossed with pasta.

4 large well-flavoured tomatoes, chopped
2 red peppers, grilled if liked, deseeded
  and chopped
2–3 chopped spring onions or 1 small red
  onion, finely chopped
1 tablespoon virgin olive oil

about 1 tablespoon balsamic vinegar to
  taste
about 2 tablespoons chopped herbs such
  as basil, chives, parsley or coriander
salt and freshly ground black pepper

Gently stir all the ingredients together.

PEPPERONI PUFFS

•

— MAKES 18 —

THESE simple savoury puffs are based on some pastries I had one Christmas at a drinks party. As I, along with everyone else that I could see, enjoyed them, I decided to try and copy the recipe.

•

225g (8oz) puff pastry
1 egg, beaten
115g (4oz) pepperoni or other spicy
   sausage, such as *chorizo*

about 15g (½oz) basil
sesame seeds

•

1. Preheat the oven to 200°C/400°F/gas 6. Roll out the pastry until it is very thin. Using a 7.5cm (3 inch) cutter, or a glass that is not too thick, stamp out 18 circles. Brush lightly with beaten egg.

2. Finely dice the sausage and tear the basil into pieces. Divide the basil and sausage between the pastry circles, placing them just off-centre. Fold the pastry over the filling to form semi-circles. Brush the tops lightly with egg and sprinkle with sesame seeds.

3. Transfer the pastries to a baking sheet and bake for 10–15 minutes. Serve hot.

SPICED NUTS AND SEEDS

So that I don't spray the nuts and seeds all over the place while I am stirring them, I use a baking tray which has raised edges, as opposed to a baking sheet, which is flat. If you don't have a baking tray, you could use a Swiss roll tin, or stir the nuts and seeds gently. They can be made in advance and kept in an airtight container for up to 2 weeks.

115g (4oz) unsalted peanuts	25g (1oz) butter, melted
50g (2oz) unsalted cashew nuts	2 teaspoons soy sauce
50g (2oz) pumpkin seeds	a few drops of Tabasco sauce
50g (2oz) sunflower seeds	$\frac{1}{2}$ teaspoon salt

1. Preheat the grill to low, or preheat the oven to 150°C/300°F/gas 2.

2. Mix all the ingredients together and spread out evenly on baking trays. Cook a little way from the grill, stirring occasionally, or in the oven, stirring once, until crisp and fragrant.

CRUNCHY CHEESE BITES

THESE are great with drinks and make a change from the usual cheese biscuits. Buy the pastry if it's more convenient than making it. The bites can be prepared in advance and left, covered, in the fridge or freezer until required, or they can be baked ahead of time and briefly warmed up in the oven before serving. The ingredients include peanuts but as it has recently come to light that some people have a severe allergic reaction to peanuts, it is a good idea to mention to guests that the biscuits contain peanuts. Alternatively, use another type of nut.

225g (8oz) shortcrust pastry
1 egg, beaten
65g (2½oz) fontina or Gruyère cheese,
   grated

paprika pepper
65g (2½oz) dry-roasted peanuts, chopped

1. Preheat the oven to 200°C/400°F/gas 6. Roll out the pastry to a 23cm (9 inch) square. Brush the pastry with beaten egg. Sprinkle the cheese over the pastry and dust with paprika pepper. Scatter the nuts over the cheese and press down firmly. Cut the pastry into six strips and gently push the strips apart.

2. Bake for about 20 minutes or until crisp and golden. Allow to cool slightly on the baking sheet, then cut into squares or triangles.

CORNMEAL MUFFINS

•

MAKES ABOUT 14

THESE are similar to American-style muffins, not traditional English yeasted muffins. I serve them as a change from bread with soups or first courses. For extra character, flavour them with herbs, finely grated Parmesan cheese or more coarsely grated Gruyère cheese, finely crumbled feta or goats' cheese, fried onion or garlic, crumbled cooked bacon, or chopped nuts, olives or sun-dried tomatoes.

115g (4oz) unsalted butter
250g (9oz) cornmeal
150g (5oz) self-raising flour
1 tablespoon baking powder

25g (1oz) sugar
2 eggs
300ml ($\frac{1}{2}$ pint) milk
salt and freshly ground black pepper

1. Preheat the oven to 200°C/400°F/gas 6. Put about 14 paper cases in a bun or muffin pan. Dice and melt the butter.

2. Stir together the cornmeal, flour, baking powder, sugar and salt and pepper. Whisk together the eggs and milk, then stir in the melted butter. Slowly pour this mixture on to the dry ingredients, stirring well to make a smooth batter.

3. Pour the batter into the paper cases and bake for about 20 minutes or until risen, golden and firm in the centre. Serve warm.

CHAPTER SIX

Desserts

WHETHER the dessert is the last part of the meal or not depends on when you serve the cheese, if, indeed, you serve cheese. I like to have the cheese between the main course and the dessert, not only when I'm serving good wines, when it makes more sense to continue with red wine before switching to a sweet white wine, but at other times because I find it confusing on the taste buds to swap from savoury to sweet, then back to savoury.

If you know that there are pudding-lovers among your guests and you want to serve a rich dessert, make sure the rest of the meal has not been too rich or heavy. If the main course has required a certain amount of attention at the last minute, I suggest that you have a dessert that is prepared in advance. If you are going to serve a dessert that requires some attention during the meal, try to prepare as much of it in advance as you can and have everything you will need ready before the meal begins.

When you are serving chilled desserts or chilled accompaniments to the dessert, such as Greek yogurt or crème fraîche, try to remember to chill the ingredients and the serving dishes. If you are going to serve ice cream as an accompaniment, do not forget to remove it from the freezer or freezing compartment to the refrigerator 20–30 minutes before it will be required. If you are serving a hot dessert, do not forget to warm the plates.

PEACH PUFFS

•

PUT the puffs in the oven to bake just before you serve the cheese course, if you have one, between the main course and the dessert. Otherwise, put them to bake as you serve the main course.

•

2 large, ripe but not soft, peaches
2 tablespoons kirsch or cognac
450g (1lb) puff pastry (or the nearest size of bought puff pastry pack)
150g (5oz) mascarpone cheese

2 large amaretti biscuits
1 egg, beaten
caster sugar for sprinkling
crème fraîche or vanilla ice cream to serve

•

1. Stone and chop the peaches and gently mix with the kirsch or cognac.

2. Roll out the pastry to a square the thickness of a 50p coin. Using a large, sharp knife, trim the edges and cut the pastry into six equal squares.

3. Divide the mascarpone between the squares, placing it in the centre of each. Top with the peaches and crumble over the amaretti. Dampen the pastry edges with water, then fold up the pastry so the corners meet in the centre. Press the edges together to seal. Transfer to a baking sheet. Put in the refrigerator for at least 20 minutes, or in the freezer for 10–15 minutes.

4. Preheat the oven to 200°C/400°F/gas 6.

5. Brush the pastry with beaten egg and bake for 15–20 minutes. Sprinkle with caster sugar and serve with crème fraîche or vanilla ice cream.

PLUM TART

·

— SERVES 6 —

THE pastry base can be baked in advance, then reheated for 3–4 minutes before completing the recipe from stage 3.

·

175g (6oz) puff pastry
675g (1½lb) ripe but firm plums
about 25g (1oz) unsalted butter
about 1½ tablespoons flaked almonds

2–3 tablespoons demerara sugar mixed
   with a pinch of ground cinnamon for
   sprinkling
real vanilla ice cream or chilled crème
   fraîche or Greek yogurt to serve

·

1. Preheat the oven to 230°C/450°F/gas 8. Roll out the pastry to a 25cm (10 inch) circle and carefully transfer to a baking sheet. Prick the surface well with a fork and bake for about 10 minutes.

2. Meanwhile, halve and stone the plums. Melt the butter.

3. Brush the pastry with butter. Arrange the plums, cut-side up, on the pastry. Bake for 20 minutes or until the plums are tender.

4. Scatter some flaked almonds over the plums, then sprinkle with the spiced sugar.

5. Return to the oven for about 10 minutes. Serve with ice cream, crème fraîche or Greek yogurt.

SOFT FRUIT TART

·

—— SERVES 6 ——

AT one time the title of this recipe would have been Summer Fruit Tart because it is topped with the types of fruit – strawberries, raspberries, etc. – that were only available in the summer months. Now, of course, they can be bought without too much difficulty virtually all the year round. These fruits do not seem to have the same flavour as our traditional summer fruits and I still tend to serve this dessert in summer rather than during the rest of the year. I sometimes add the pulp and seeds from one or two passion fruit as well.

The size of the filo pastry sheets doesn't matter because they can easily be arranged and cut if necessary so that they cover the base of the flan tin entirely, and any loose ends that fall over the sides of the tin can be left, tucked in slightly or trimmed a little; they need not be flush with the rim of the flan tin. The filling is lusciously rich; if you want to make it lighter use low-fat soft cheese instead of most of the crème fraîche. The pastry case and the filling can both be made in advance.

·

50g (2oz) unsalted butter
about 115g (4oz) filo pastry
200g (7oz) mascarpone cheese, chilled
a few drops of vanilla essence
grated zest of 1 lemon

225ml (8fl oz) crème fraîche, chilled
about 700g (1½lb) mixed summer fruits,
   such as strawberries, raspberries,
   blackberries, blueberries, peaches
icing sugar for dusting (optional)

·

1. Preheat the oven to 200°C/400°F/gas 6. Melt the butter and brush a little over the base and sides of a 23cm (9 inch) loose-bottomed flan tin. Layer the pastry in the tin, brushing each sheet with butter and overlapping the sheets so there are no gaps. Bake for 12–15 minutes or until crisp and golden. Remove the outer ring, and slip off the base, if liked (it hastens cooling) and leave to cool.

2. Meanwhile, beat together the mascarpone cheese, vanilla essence to taste, and the lemon zest. Return to the fridge.

3. Prepare the fruits as necessary – halve, quarter or slice the strawberries, and stone and slice the peaches.

4. Spread the cheese mixture in the pastry case and top with the fruit. Dust with icing sugar, if liked, and serve.

Apricot and Amaretti Crumble

·

THE crumble mixture can be prepared in advance and kept in a covered container in the fridge. The dish can be cooked on a lower shelf of the oven when any of the roast lamb recipes, or the Italian Roast Chicken and Vegetables (see page 48) are cooking, or it could go into the oven after baking the Crisp and Melting Tomato and Mozzarella Filo Pastries (see page 14) or the Cheese Puffs (see page 13).

900g (2lb) ripe but firm apricots
about 2 tablespoons sugar

CRUMBLE
50g (2oz) unsalted butter
75g (3oz) plain flour
25g (1oz) sugar
115g (4oz) amaretti biscuits

APRICOT SAUCE (optional)
about 115g (4oz) sugar
225ml (8fl oz) orange juice
2 tablespoons lemon juice
1 vanilla pod, halved lengthways
   (optional)
small piece of cinnamon, broken
4 tablespoons crème fraîche

1. Preheat the oven to 180°C/350°F/gas 4. Reserve four apricots if making the sauce. Thickly slice the remainder and put into a baking dish. Toss with the sugar.

2. To make the crumble, chop and then rub the butter into the flour and sugar until the mixture resembles coarse breadcrumbs. Crush the amaretti over the mixture and stir in. Sprinkle over the apricots. Bake for 20–25 minutes or until the apricots are soft and the crumble browned.

3. Meanwhile, chop the reserved apricots and simmer with the sugar, orange and lemon juices, vanilla pod and cinnamon until tender. Scoop out the vanilla, if used, and the cinnamon, and purée the sauce in a blender. Stir in the crème fraîche. Serve with the crumble.

CHOCOLATE AMARETTO CASTLES

•

—— SERVES 6 ——

THESE are steamed puddings but they are much lighter and more sophisticated than traditional steamed puddings. This is a good recipe for the occasions when you want to serve a hot pudding that can be left to cook unattended, yet do not want to use the oven. If you have a favourite chocolate sauce recipe, you can use that instead of the one given here.

•

175g (6oz) plain flour
3 tablespoons cocoa powder
40g (1½oz) ground almonds
150g (5oz) caster sugar
75g (3oz) soft margarine
2 eggs, beaten

4½ tablespoons amaretto liqueur
milk (optional)

SAUCE
350g (12oz) chocolate and hazelnut
  spread
finely grated zest and juice of 1 small
  orange

•

1. Lightly oil and flour six dariole moulds or ramekin dishes and put in a saucepan, flameproof dish or small roasting tin. Pour water around the moulds or dishes to come halfway up the sides and heat the water to simmering.

2. Beat all the pudding ingredients, except the milk, together with a hand-held electric whisk (or use a food processor or food mixer) until the mixture is smooth. If necessary, add a little milk to make a soft dropping consistency.

3. Divide the mixture between the moulds or dishes. Lay a sheet of greaseproof paper loosely over the top of the moulds or dishes. Cover with a lid and steam for 25–30 minutes. Keep an eye on the water level and top up if necessary.

4. To make the sauce, gently warm the spread with the orange zest and juice, stirring until smooth. Serve with the unmoulded puddings.

SPECIAL PEACH BRÛLÉES

·

—— SERVES 6 ——

B RÛLÉES have been popular desserts for quite a number of years. Some are 'healthy', with a yogurt topping, while some are richer, with cream. From the cook's point of view, they are ideal for a dinner party because they are easy to prepare and quick to cook, and always well received. They can also be prepared in advance, if liked, then put in the fridge when completely cold. This is an extra special version that will be even better received because it includes brandy and amaretti biscuits, and has crème fraîche as a topping. If you want to make it even more luxurious, mix mascarpone cheese with the crème fraîche.

6 ripe peaches
2–3 tablespoons brandy
3–4 amaretti biscuits

425ml (15fl oz) crème fraîche
115–150g (4–5oz) soft light brown sugar

1. Preheat the grill to hot. Halve and stone the peaches and slice into six large individual ramekin dishes. Sprinkle over a little brandy. Coarsely crush the amaretti over the top and cover with a thick layer of crème fraîche.

2. Sprinkle over the sugar to cover the crème fraîche completely. Grill until caramelised.

GLAZED PEARS

•

— SERVES 6 —

IF you have time and the inclination, make a nice buttery Madeira cake (it's very easy) and bake it in a loaf tin. If you do not have time the day before the dinner, the cake can be made in advance and frozen, but don't forget to take it out of the freezer the night or morning before the dinner.

•

1 small Madeira cake	3 small ripe Williams pears
about 4 tablespoons kirsch	25g (1oz) unsalted butter, melted
mascarpone cheese for spreading	1–1½ tablespoons light soft brown sugar

•

1. Preheat the grill. Cut the cake into six slices about 5mm (¼ inch) thick. Put on a heatproof serving plate, or six individual heatproof plates. Sprinkle with kirsch and spread with the mascarpone cheese.

2. Thinly slice the pears and arrange, slightly overlapping, on the cake. Brush with melted butter. Sprinkle with sugar and grill for about 10 minutes or until pale gold.

COCONUT CUSTARDS

.

—— SERVES 6 ——

Serve these custards warm or cold with sliced mango or papaya.

.

570ml (1 pint) coconut milk

about 65g (2½oz) sugar

4 eggs

4 egg yolks

toasted coconut flakes or desiccated

coconut for decoration

.

1. Preheat the oven to 170°C/325°F/gas 3. Put six ramekin dishes in a roasting tin. Bring a kettle of water to the boil.

2. Gently heat the coconut milk and sugar.

3. Beat the eggs and egg yolks together. Pour the milk on to the eggs, whisking to mix. Strain or pour into the dishes.

4. Pour boiling water around the dishes to come two thirds of the way up the sides. Cook in the oven for 20–30 minutes or until only just set. Serve with toasted coconut or dessicated coconut sprinkled over.

GINGER POTS

•

THE piquancy of the preserved ginger gives a clean, refreshing taste to these smooth, creamy custards. They can be served warm or cold.

570ml (1 pint) milk or milk and cream

1 vanilla pod

2½ tablespoons finely chopped preserved
   ginger

about 65g (2½oz) sugar

4 eggs

4 egg yolks

1. Preheat the oven to 170°C/325°F/gas 3. Put six ramekin dishes in a roasting tin. Bring a kettle of water to the boil.

2. Gently heat the milk. Split the vanilla pod lengthways and scrape the seeds into the milk. Add the pod, ginger and sugar to the milk.

3. Beat the eggs and egg yolks together. Strain them if liked. Pour the milk on to the eggs, whisking to mix. Discard the vanilla pod. Divide the custard between the dishes.

4. Pour boiling water around the dishes to come two thirds of the way up the sides, and put the roasting tin in the oven. Cook for 20–30 minutes or until only just set.

LIME SYLLABUB

·

SERVE the syllabub on its own, in elegant glasses, or serve it over fruit such as strawberries, ripe peaches or pears.

·

finely grated zest and juice of 2 limes
115ml (4fl oz) dessert wine, such as
  Beaumes de Venise or moscatel
about 50g (2oz) caster sugar

300ml (½ pint) double cream
150g (5oz) Greek yogurt
1 egg white
crisp biscuits to serve

·

1. Mix together the lime zest and juice, the wine and half the sugar. Leave for 15 minutes, if possible, to allow the flavours to infuse.

2. Whisk the cream and yogurt together until they form stiff peaks. Stir in the wine mixture and whisk again until the mixture holds its shape.

3. Using a clean whisk, whisk the egg white until stiff. Lightly whisk in the remaining sugar, then lightly fold into the cream mixture using a large metal spoon. Divide between four cold serving glasses or dishes, and serve straight away accompanied by crisp biscuits.

MANGO AND BANANA FOOL

•

— SERVES 6 —

THE exotic and everyday are quickly and easily combined in this luxurious-tasting dessert.

1 ripe mango, peeled, flesh removed from stone and coarsely chopped
4 ripe bananas, peeled and coarsely chopped

grated zest and juice of 1 large lime
2 tablespoons sugar, preferably vanilla-flavoured
300ml ($\frac{1}{2}$ pint) double cream, chilled

1. Mix the mango, bananas, lime juice and sugar together in a blender or food processor.

2. Whip the cream until it stands in soft peaks, then gently fold in the mango mixture in three or four batches.

3. Divide between six cold, tall glasses and chill until required. Sprinkle over the lime zest before serving.

SPICED AND BUTTERED PLUMS

•

THE plums do have to be cooked at the last minute but they only take 10 minutes (you can have all the ingredients ready) and by the end of a meal such a short break won't be noticed. If a partner or co-operative friend clears the table, by the time that is done the dessert will be ready to make its spectacular entrance.

675g (1½lb) dark plums
75g (3oz) unsalted butter, diced
115g (4oz) sugar, or to taste

about ½ teaspoon ground cinnamon
3 tablespoons brandy
crème fraîche or vanilla ice cream to serve

---

1. Cut the plums in half following the natural indentations. Discard the stones.

2. Melt the butter in a large frying pan and add the plums, cut-side up, in a single layer. Sprinkle over the sugar and cinnamon, cover and cook gently for 5 minutes. Turn the plums over, shake the pan if necessary to dissolve the sugar, cover again and cook for a further 5 minutes.

3. Warm the brandy in a small saucepan over a low heat; do not allow to boil.

4. Tip the plums and their cooking juices into a warm, shallow, flameproof serving dish. Set the brandy alight and pour, still flaming, over the plums. Take carefully to the table before the flames subside. Serve with crème fraîche or vanilla ice cream.

BAKED BUTTERY SPICED BANANAS

•

—— SERVES 6 ——

SIMILAR recipes are often cooked on the hob, but this does mean they need last-minute attention; if in the oven, the bananas can be left to cook while you enjoy the rest of the meal.

6 ripe but firm bananas
juice of 3 oranges
juice of 1 lemon

4 tablespoons rum
seeds from 5 cardamom pods, crushed
115g (4oz) unsalted butter, diced

1. Preheat the oven to 200°C/400°F/gas 6. Peel the bananas, cut in half across the middle, then slice each length in half. Put in a shallow baking dish.

2. Pour the fruit juices and rum over the bananas. Sprinkle with the cardamom seeds and dot with the butter.

3. Bake in the oven for about 20 minutes, basting the bananas a couple of times, until they are just soft. Serve straight away.

CHERRY COMPOTE

·

—— SERVES 6 ——

THIS compote needs to be prepared long enough before the meal to allow it to cool. Adjust the sweetness according to the sweetness of the cherries and your taste; it is better to err on the side of undersweetening and to serve a bowl of brown sugar separately. I prefer to use potato starch (available from health food shops), which thickens instantly and does not need cooking through, or arrowroot (available from chemists), rather than corn-flour as the first two produce a clear, lightly thickened sauce whereas cornflour makes it cloudy and gluey and needs to be cooked. Serve with cool Greek yogurt, real vanilla ice cream or clotted cream.

300ml (½ pint) medium-bodied red wine
about 50g (2oz) caster sugar to taste
grated zest of 1 orange
1 cinnamon stick, broken

600g (1¼lb) ripe cherries, stones removed
1½ teaspoons potato starch or arrowroot
3 tablespoons kirsch

1. Put the wine, sugar, orange zest and cinnamon into a saucepan and bring to the boil over a low heat, stirring, until the sugar is dissolved.

2. Add the cherries and return to the boil.

3. Slake the potato starch or arrowroot with a little cold water and stir into the pan. Heat, stirring gently, until just thickened. Add the kirsch. Pour into a serving bowl and leave to cool.

4. Discard the cinnamon and serve.

NO-COOK DRIED FRUIT COMPOTE

•

—— SERVES 6 ——

THIS dessert is ideal when the rest of the menu requires a certain amount of attention, or you are really pushed for time, because no cooking is needed. You do have to plan in advance, though, because the fruit has to be left to marinate for 36–48 hours. If there is not time to leave the fruit for $1\frac{1}{2}$–2 days, warm the fruit juice until very hot, but not boiling, before pouring it over the fruit.

675g (1½lb) mixed dried fruits, such as
    pears, peaches, figs, apricots, apples,
    mangoes and prunes
1 cinnamon stick
seeds from 6 cardamom pods, crushed
4 star anise

1 bay leaf, torn
1.7 litres (3 pints) mixed apple and orange
    juice
cool crème fraîche, mascarpone cheese or
    Greek yogurt to serve

---

1. Put the fruit and spices in a bowl. Stir in the fruit juice, cover and leave in a cool place, preferably not the refrigerator, for 36–48 hours, stirring occasionally.

2. Serve with cool crème fraîche, mascarpone cheese or Greek yogurt.

Index

accompaniments, 83–104
almonds: spinach, pecorino cheese and almond salad, 6
amaretti biscuits: apricot and amaretti crumble, 109
apples: pork collops with cranberry and apple relish, 78
   pork noisettes with apple and sage relish, 79
   venison with cranberry and apple relish, 61
apricot and amaretti crumble, 109
artichokes: artichoke and sun-dried tomato ragout, 92
   pork collops with artichokes and mushrooms, 77
Asian-inspired prawn and avocado salad, 16
asparagus soup, 5
aubergines: baked baby aubergines, 90
   lamb with Middle-Eastern aubergine purée, 73
avocados: Asian-inspired prawn and avocado salad, 16
   chicken and avocado stroganoff with pesto, 55
   grilled prawns with spiced avocado sauce, 22
   prawn and monkfish kebabs with tomato and avocado salsa, 24

bananas: baked buttery spiced bananas, 118
   mango and banana fool, 116
basil: grilled salmon steaks with tomatoes and basil, 31
   noisettes of lamb with two tomato and basil sauce, 71
   pesto, 98
   warm prawn and basil salad, 12
bass with ginger vinaigrette, 29
Béarnaise sauce, steaks with, 65
beef, 63

beef and broccoli stir-fry, 67
   sautéed whole fillet of beef with Chinese marinade, 64
   steaks with Béarnaise sauce, 65
   steaks with horseradish relish, 66
biscuits: crunchy cheese bites, 103
brill: brill with fragrant coconut sauce, 41
   Provençal brill fillet rolls, 40
brioches with prawns, 23
British veal kebab rolls, 68
broccoli: beef and broccoli stir-fry, 67
   broccoli with olive oil hollandaise sauce, 89
butter, xi
butter bean purée, 88

cannellini beans: white beans with salsa verde, 87
carrots: carrot timbales with quick ginger hollandaise, 25
   spiced carrot soup, 2
casserole, Mediterranean fish, 45
cheese: cheese puffs, 13
   crisp and melting tomato and mozzarella filo pastries, 14
   crunchy cheese bites, 103
   pork roulades with feta and herb filling, 80
   spinach, pecorino cheese and almond salad, 6
   turkey rolls with pesto and mozzarella cheese, 56
cherry compote, 119
chicken, 47
   baked chicken in coconut sauce, 53
   baked sesame chicken, 52
   chicken and avocado stroganoff with pesto, 55
   fragrant chicken, 54
   grilled chicken with vermouth and lime, 51
   Italian roast chicken and vegetables, 48